Tales From Sales

Tales From Sales

❖

Outrageous, Hilarious and True Stories From Home Sales

Myka Allen-Johnson

Library of Congress Control Number: 2013900382
ISBN: Hardcover   978-1-4797-7573-6
                         Softcover   978-1-4797-7572-9
                         Ebook   978-1-4797-7574-3

This book was printed in the United States of America.

To order additional copies of this book, contact:
Xlibris Corporation
1-888-795-4274
www.Xlibris.com

CONTENTS

Part I

The Hilarious and Ridiculous

Part II

Elvis Presley The King Lived in Killeen, Texas So . . . I Bought His House

Part III

Military Matters

Part IV

Partner Parables

Part V

Shorties but Goodies!

This book is dedicated to my family.
Kyle, thank you for your love, patience,
and putting up with these crazy stories
all the time. Mazzy, you are the love of my
life, the reason I live. Mom, Dad, and
Marla, thank you for a lifetime of love,
laughter, and God's word.

"The family. We were a strange little band of characters trudging through life sharing diseases and toothpaste, coveting one another's desserts, hiding shampoo, borrowing money, locking each other out of our rooms, inflicting pain and kissing to heal it in the same instant, loving, laughing, defending, and trying to figure out the common thread that bound us all together."

—Erma Bombeck

"Love is patient and kind; love does not envy or boast; it is not arrogant or rude. It does not insist on its own way; it is not irritable or resentful; it does not rejoice at wrongdoing, but rejoices with the truth. Love bears all things, believes all things, hopes all things, endures all things."

—Corinthians 13:4-7

ACCLAIM FOR THE AUTHOR

"I have had the opportunity to be a part of Myka's work career, and she is such a great storyteller! Through her years of home sales experiences, she has 'hit the nail on the head' with her humor, wit, and attention to details. These stories make you laugh, cry, and realize what people in our industry go through on the 'average' day. If you like a good read and you love a good sense of humor, these stories are for you!"

—Chris Werth, Division President, Ashton Woods Homes

"Tales from Sales is laugh-out-loud funny! Myka has a special talent for noticing all the hilarious happenings of everyday life. Then again, she may be just one of those people who attract those crazy and strange 'you'll never believe what happened' situations! Either way, you're going to love this book; no interest in sales necessary. I've known Myka a very long time, and reading her book is just like spending time with her . . . you'll laugh until you cry!"

—Denise Weathers, Teacher

"A great read, no matter what profession you are in! I couldn't wait to see who would walk in her office door next! Informative and entertaining! I will definitely make this part of my personal collection!"

—Sandy Davis, GISD Librarian

"Wow! We give this book an A+! We laughed and laughed at the stories because they hit so close to home. The story about the trailer house was absolutely hilarious; I could just picture the characters and the ridiculous stack of vacuums! Well written, very funny, and such a true picture of real estate today. This one's a keeper!"

—Marla Ray, Teacher

"Vastly entertaining . . . nonstop hilarity . . . a must read for those who work every day in the real estate world as well for those who have no idea what a roller coaster there is in sales!

No one could imagine that the selling of real estate would be such a hoot!"

—Sarah Edwards

"Incredibly delightful! Who would have thought that real estate agents could have this much fun? And all from the woman who sold Elvis's home!

Need a lift? Some light bathroom literature for those special quiet times? A coffee table book for Sunday afternoons when the Cowboys are breaking your heart (yet again)?

Try Tales from Sales. *You'll love it!"*

—Bill Fowler, Professor at Howard Payne University

"Fabulously entertaining stories! I've laughed right to tears. Hilarious and fun to read! Keep 'em coming, Myka!"

—Samantha Jackson, Loan Officer

"I love these stories! Having been in the business for years, I can definitely relate. And your writing is so entertaining. Thank you for the laughs!"

—Teresa Adams, Broker and Brokerage Owner

"Oh my god! I just can't wait for the next story to be posted. I love reading these and because I have known Myka for so long, I can just picture her sitting there in front of me telling me what happened. I can so vividly see the expression she would make. These are the best; keep them coming. My sides hurt from laughing so much.

Keep up the amazing tales, Myka."

—GiGi Martinez

"A wonderful and refreshing book of life experiences as told by the author.

I imagined I had just met her for lunch and listened as she painted word pictures of the situations she has lived. She openly shares her life lessons. Definitely a good read."

—Charlotte Leifester

"As a real estate professional, I find the writings of Myka's blog to be so humorous! Many of the tips are so helpful to agents who are newer to our industry. The funniest thing about the blogs is the fact that these events actually happened! Keep writing, Myka, your style is unique and real, and we really enjoy reading your blogs!"

—Linda Carey, Realtor

Photo by: Micah Jalbert

PREFACE

I didn't go to school originally for real estate. I went to college to be a Spanish teacher and volleyball coach. I was a sheltered preacher's daughter who went to a private Christian school. It never crossed my mind that my entire life would revolve around real estate until my fifth year of teaching. I knew that my calling was to teach and train. So inside those five years of teaching were wonderful experiences, but there were also some eye-opening scary ones. I was sheltered, but I knew that the things I was experiencing weren't the norm for a teacher. I had a huge chunk of my hair torn out, my clothes torn, my thumb broken, my life threatened, and my dog's life threatened, among many other things.

The mind-set for my career started to change the day when my life was threatened, and the boy who threatened it also said that he would shoot my dog. I let another teacher watch my class, and I was going directly to that students' home to have a serious talk with his parents. Before I left, I had told my principal what had happened, but he said the boy hadn't had any other offenses and that it would probably be okay, which was why I took things into my own hands and was on my way to have a talk with the parental units. No one threatens to kill me or my dog!

Upon arrival at the boy's home, I was even more scared when I realized how close he lived to my house. It was literally the next block down. When I knocked on the front door, the father answered.

I introduced myself and told him what happened and how his son had threatened my life and my dog. After hearing the news, he threw his head back and laughed a hearty laugh. He said, "He's not going shoot you or anyone. We took his gun away from him yesterday. He got in trouble for shooting neighborhood dogs, but he doesn't have a gun anymore."

I realized what I was dealing with and that teaching and really making a difference was an uphill battle. I was working over eighty hours a week with coaching and teaching combined and was still making poverty-level paychecks. There were many days that I sat in an apartment with no power and no phone because after the day I got paid, I literally had $200 to make it to the end of the month. I have the utmost respect for our teachers and hope that one day they get the pay they deserve!

One day, I had just had enough; and I had been praying constantly, asking for God to lead me and help me know what to do. It came to me that day, and I just knew. I put in my letter of resignation. I had no other job to go to. Nothing else on the horizon. But I instantly knew that I couldn't and I didn't want to teach anymore.

I left school that day and drove around in a daze. What was I going to do? How was I going to make ends meet? My dad, the preacher and theology professor with two doctorates, was so proud of me for following in his footsteps. How do I tell him I'm done?

As I was driving around in my own fog, it was a cloudy and rainy day, but I still felt like a weight had lifted off me and that I was on the right track. But there was still the problem of not knowing what to do for a job. So as I was driving, my attention was suddenly grabbed by a single bright ray of sunshine shining through the rain clouds and splitting the fog. It was literally shining only on a small sign I had driven by dozens of times and never noticed, on the right side of the road, which said, "Get Your Real Estate License Here."

I couldn't believe it! Was this my sign? I pulled in, went inside, and talked to the broker of the real estate company and told her I had been a teacher and knew that wasn't the right career for me. I had never thought of real estate but had prayed for a sign. I literally got my sign!

I started my classes, I got my license, and the rest is history! Here I am, writing a book about the craziest experiences in my real estate career. In this book, you will hear stories from when I was practicing general real estate as a Realtor®, and then there are many stories from when I worked with a Fortune 500 builder as a new home sales professional and then as a national sales trainer and consultant.

My parents raised me in a Christian environment, and they also raised me to have a sense of humor about life in general. For a preacher, Dad always had to go to sick people's bedsides and counsel sad, depressed, or problem-plagued church members. The church is always full of drama. Good and bad. I am a Christian, but I have learned and know that if you don't have a sense of humor, you'll drown!

So I had a hilarious childhood filled with practical jokes, funny family nights, games, stories, and just plain fun. All of my friends wanted to come to my house on weekends instead of going out because we always had fun there. My family taught me to look at everything positively and find the bright side or the funny in it. I did.

I guess you could say my first crazy real estate experience happened when I was a freshman in high school in Brownwood, Texas. As a preacher's daughter, we were able to stay in what is called a parsonage, which is a home that the church buys for the preacher and his family to stay in. We had been in a parsonage from the time I was in kindergarten until high school.

On my freshman year, Dad started to preach for a different church that was much smaller and did not have a parsonage. So for the first time ever, we were going to buy a home. We got a realtor and began looking for homes in Brownwood. We looked at several houses, but only one gave me my first scary and crazy experience in real estate.

I remember everything like it was a movie I just watched. We pulled into the driveway of a modest little three-bedroom home on a busy street. I noticed that the garage door was up just a little bit the way we would always leave it for the cats to come into the garage. The realtor made an offhand comment that the owner was an elderly man who didn't live there anymore, and she hoped that he wasn't here getting some remaining items. I guess because it would be awkward. Boy, was she ever right!

Mom said something about checking to make sure there was a car in the garage, so I got down on my stomach and looked inside the garage through the six-inch gap, and sure enough . . . I saw tires. The owner was there.

We rang the doorbell. Rang it again and started knocking and looking through windows to see if anyone was home. We all just assumed that maybe the owner had left his car here and gone with someone else in order for us to view the home. So . . . the realtor stuck her key in the lock, turned the knob, and opened the door. She screamed and nearly ran over all of us! The front door was flung open; and I swear to you, a swarm of thousands of the biggest, fattest flies flew into us, hitting our faces and pummeling us as they flew past us and out of the house. The screen door slammed, and thousands upon thousands of flies were hitting the screen door trying to get out. Then . . . the smell.

That smell somehow remains in your memory no matter how much time passes. It was sweet and horribly sickening. We all started gagging and were absolutely positive about what was inside the house now. We were all so sickened that we were forced to move out to the street. We called the police, and I'll never forget this as long as I live; the policeman went in like he was some kind of tough guy. No mask or anything. The next thing we saw was him running out and throwing up in the bushes outside the door.

Sadly, the owner had died in the bathroom of the home and had been dead for over a week. If that many flies were trying to get out of there, I cannot even imagine what the scene was like in the bathroom. The policeman said that we did not want to know. That event forever marked the beginning of a long line of crazy and outrageous stories that would start again after I moved away from home, finished school, quit teaching, and became a realtor.

I started selling in Dallas, Texas, but moved to Killeen, Texas, shortly thereafter to be with my husband who had grown up here. I grew up only minutes from Killeen, but I had never been here! I knew nothing about the town when I moved here, but everyone said it was a great real estate market, and it was and it still is.

The very heartbeat of Killeen is that the largest military installation in the world, Fort Hood, is here. Killeen is a melting pot boiling over with the bravest of military heroes and people who have come here from all over the world. There are over 120,000 people in Killeen alone, and that's not even counting the many communities surrounding it in Central Texas. Elvis Presley even lived here in 1958, and I bought the house he lived in. That story is included as well!

Everywhere you go, there are soldiers in army greens. I'm so glad that I moved here because I would have never understood what a soldier and the soldier's family goes through. I have written a few stories about some of the bravest people I have ever met, and I'm so thankful that Killeen has given me the chance to see those heroes in action.

After ten years of sales, I came home every day to my husband and told him the crazy stories of ridiculous events that had transpired. After every sales function, a storytelling session ensued, and these same stories had taken a living, breathing life of their own, and some stories have become famous, even legendary around Central Texas among all of the real estate professionals. We have laughed so hard at these stories over the years that they all begged me to write them down in a book.

You will notice in this book that most parts of it I have written exactly what people have said, even down to the accents and misuse of words. I've tried to replace some bad words with better words or leave a few letters blank so you'll know exactly what these hilarious people said without me saying it. If I didn't say *exactly* what they said and how they said it, it wouldn't be funny. So please don't take offense.

I didn't realize how many stories I had until I started to put them down on paper. I have picked the funniest and the best stories for this book, and I hope that you enjoy it! I love my job, I love my clients, and I even love the crazy ones. After all these years, I have opened my own brokerage and have a whole new set of unbelievable stories. The characters keep on coming, and the stories keep getting better too!

I've met many characters in my sales career so far, and that's really the only way to describe them: characters. I have changed the names of all the characters in this book to protect the innocent and the guilty.

The majority of my transactions are normal . . . but after over ten years, I've chosen the craziest and most outrageous and hilarious stories for this book! I hope you laugh as hard as I did. Enjoy.

PART I
The Hilarious and Ridiculous

Chickens and Goats and Kittens! Oh my!

Recently, I took a nice young lady to see some property in a neighboring town with a population of about 1,200. It was a small town; cute little area and very rural. It was 107 degrees outside that day, and it had been over 100 degrees for the last sixty days. Showing homes was definitely not a fun event this particular summer. I told my customer, Janis, to meet me at the home and the listing realtor would meet us there to open it. When we arrived, it's only me and my client, Janis. No listing realtor.

I call the listing realtor, and he says, "Oh, I can't go but the owner is going to open the door and give you a tour."

"A tour?" I asked. It's a mobile home on two acres. I'm sure we can figure it out!

"Yes." The listing realtor continued. "Oh, and by the way . . . don't look at what the lady has done to the house, just think about what it could be," he said and hung up abruptly.

Uh oh. That usually means that the place is in deplorable condition and if your client wants to spend a boatload of money, they can make it look habitable. It's like those listings with the roof caving in, water pooling in the middle of the floor from a slab leak, the post mortem remains of a squatter who took his final nap in the bedroom, and the listing realtor proudly announces that it's, "As is. A fixer-upper. Handyman special!"

There's not enough "fixin'" in the world that can do what renting a bulldozer can! But this house doesn't look too bad on the outside. If you look beyond the twelve terrifying scarecrows that are scattered around the yard (that aren't guarding any sort of crop or vegetation and just look like a scary dead guy hanging from a stick), the weird gothic fountains with no water and piles of trash everywhere, you could see a little promise of a humble abode.

I step out of the car, and at the same time, Janis steps out as well. This is my first time to meet her in person so we exchange pleasantries. I've learned a long time ago that one person's nightmare home could be another person's dream, so I say nothing of the Tim Burton moviescape that is the front yard and we make our way to the front porch.

Just as we reach the rickety wood front porch with three barbeque pits on it, the door opens and out staggers a portly woman in her sixties or seventies wearing a tube top dress that the sun was shining straight through; allowing us a view of what God has so bountifully blessed her with. I avert my eyes and look at her face in order to make eye contact and initiate a hello and a handshake.

I try not to act shocked when the lady in the tube dress has a full mustache and patchy scruff for a beard. I silently curse hormones in my head and promise to put money aside for laser hair removal for eternity.

"Hello! Your realtor says you're going to help us out today? I'm Myka. It's nice to meet you."

"It's hotter'n hades out there. Ya'll come on in. It's not very clean but you can do whatever you want to it when you buy it. My cat just runned away and I'm perty sad. I hope she don't run off with no pack of wild cats and never come back." She started to get a little misty eyed and her voice broke.

"I'm sorry," I said, trying to break the silence and also to keep her from starting to cry. "Maybe she went under the house. She'll come back. I bet nobody loves her or feeds her like you."

"Why she runned off then, you think?" she asked in a desperate tone with pleading eyes.

"Oh. Who knows? But she'll be back. Do you want to show us around or can we wander around ourselves?" I asked.

At this point, I was trying to figure out what the musty smell was. It was irritatingly sweet and sour at the same time. I was stifling a gag. Janis, my client, said absolutely nothing and was just staring at a wall in front of her.

"Pack'a wild dogs ate up mah air conditioner. That's why it's so hot. Ya'll can look around if you'd like. I ain't got nothing to hide," she said as she searched out the window for her prodigal kitty.

Janis was attached to my hip and we moved around like a two-headed beast trying not to touch anything. I started in the kitchen and looked up above the cabinet and saw another scary sight that made me want to just go back out to the car and burn rubber on the way out of there. It was a two-foot statue of the grim reaper with several other little reapers around it. I was so uncomfortable that I made a comment about it.

"Oh! Look at that. That's different for a kitchen décor." Oh gosh! Why did I say that? That's great! Make her mad and she'll put some weird voodoo scarecrow spell on me.

"Oh, that's my little friend," she said, not even really paying attention to us.

There's just enough room on the floor for us to go room to room in a conga line. The master bedroom had carpet, and there were urine stains all over the floor and an ammonia smell. I was trying not to hurt this lady's feeling by going in and out quickly, but I was having a hard time keeping the contents of my stomach in my stomach.

Next, we meandered to the guest rooms, and the first one had a bunch of furniture stacked on top of each other up to the ceiling and about eighteen to twenty vacuum cleaners. Again, I should have kept my mouth shut, but I was just nervously talking at this point. I said, "Oh wow. Look at all these vacuum cleaners. Why do you have so many?"

She sighed and said, "Well . . . you seen them chickens out thar in the chicken coop? Before I had the money for a coop they used to stay in this room, and I'd just vacuum up their mess every day. I don't know how to fix a vacuum, so I just bought a new one every time one would clog up."

Well, that's a first! Raising chickens inside the house. I have never seen that one until now. I just acted like that was normal and continued the tour. We finally finished inside, and she started to show us the boundaries of the property. I was just thanking God we were outside. She had a few goats behind the fence, and one of them came running up to the fence bleating with excitement upon seeing the owner of the home.

"Hey! Momma's here!" she baby talked the little goat. "You see that thar goat? I raised her from a little baby with a bottle right thar in mah living room. She lived with me for a year until she was strong enough to go outside on her own. That's my baby."

Oh, for god's sake! Goats and chickens inside the house! They didn't even do that on *Little House on the Prairie*! I keep looking at Janis for any sort of emotion, and she's been silent the whole time. I bet she's mortified. I am!

We finish the tour as the owner loses interest in us and wanders off calling her lost kitty cat. Janis and I walk over to our cars, and I say, "Wow!" with a shocked look on my face.

"I know," Janis says. "So should we make an offer today or make them wait a little?"

Huh? I thought she was joking. She wasn't.

"I really like it. Maybe we can get a good deal. Let's start low and see what happens."

I'm still in shock and waiting for her to bust out laughing and say, "Gotcha!" No such luck.

"Okay," I said slowly. "We'll definitely want to get an inspector out here to make sure it's a good investment."

"Yeah. Good idea. You call the inspector and we can go write up the contract," she said excitedly.

As I stared unbelievingly at a gothic scarecrow swaying in the breeze, I realized that it's never my opinion that counts. Everyone has their own dream home even if livestock was raised inside of it. Even if the grim reaper watches over you while you do your dishes and even if every kid in town is scared to tears by your front yard; to each their own. Long live the American dream!

EIGHTEEN G's!

When I first moved to Killeen, I began selling homes for a local builder who had several beautiful model homes around town. At the time, I managed to be able to work in the most popular sales model in town. So people would come in and out of the model home like it was a normal business. Sundays were very busy and always very interesting!

One beautiful Sunday afternoon, I was expecting the usual Sunday crowd of after church goers. My take on this phenomenon is that people get to dress up in their flashiest duds, go to church, show off for an hour, and maybe go out to eat and parade around the restaurant in giant hats and splendid shades of bright purple, hot pink, and lime green. As is the case in all parades, we're all sad when it's over. So I believe that these Sunday after church goers just wanted to extend the parade a little longer, show off their nicest clothes, and waste their time looking at model homes. Of course, that's just my theory now that I've been selling for so long and have seen it happen every Sunday for ten years. Ask any seasoned sales veteran; they'll tell you the same thing.

On that beautiful Sunday afternoon, I opened the door to let the parade in. First to walk through the door were several adorable little three-foot tall boys in full three-piece suits. Following them were three grown men who were dressed exactly like the little boys but with big boy suits on that were "LA Lakers purple." Bringing up the rear was a sight that even Martin Lawrence or Eddie Murphy couldn't portray in one of their movies about overweight mommas! The largest woman I have still ever seen to this day, dressed in a hot pink wrap dress and a hot pink hat with feathers on it that could provide shade for all her boys to sit under. She literally had to take off her hat to get through the door.

In addition to her breathtaking style, she had no shoes on. As I was trying to grasp the fact that she was walking into a public place of business with no shoes, my mind was suddenly trying to wrap itself around the sight of her toes sticking out of giant holes in her stockings. As my eyes "elevatored" themselves up from her feet to her knees, again my breath was taken as I saw that her last visit to the leg waxer had been several years prior and the years had taken their toll as the hairs were trying to break free of a pantyhose prison.

Suddenly, my gaze from momma was broken when the closest of the three brothers in a three-piece suit said, "Say, what's the biggest house ya'll selling up in here? I'm looking for about twenty to thirty thousand square feet. Whatcha got?"

Now I'm from New Orleans, Louisiana, and even this was a thick southern drawl! But I can spot a fellow "Nawlins" native just after a few words!

Trying to lighten the atmosphere a little, mainly because I still had a look of shock on my face and I wanted to gently let him know that twenty or thirty thousand square feet is a ridiculous-sized house, I said, "Well, if you're looking for something *that* large, I think the local football stadium is for sale!"

Then the room echoed with only my laughter and my attempt at humor had completely failed, and I cleared my throat and said, "I think you mean two or three thousand square feet."

He said, "Yeah . . . yeah. That's what I meant. I want to buy the biggest house you got. I'm gonna buy it fo' my momma."

After he said this, Momma, in her pink Sunday dress, came alive and started clapping and flapping her arms. She began chanting, "My baby gon' buy momma a house! Baby gon' buy momma a house! Praise the Lord! Hallelujah! My baby gon' buy me a house!" Then she grabbed her son, absorbed him into her flesh, and gave him a big motherly hug.

From experience, generally anyone who comes in asking for the biggest house we sell or the largest lot we sell, doesn't ever think that money is an issue, but it usually is an issue. So I asked them all to come to my office so we could talk about the financials and see how much of a home they qualify for. Let me just add that my office was about nine foot by nine foot and it was the middle of July in Texas. So all of us "Nawlins" natives (eight to be exact, including me) packed into my office and I start choking down my claustrophobia. Let the qualifying process begin:

"Our largest home is about 3,200 square feet and usually sells for around $200,000," I said.

"Yeah, dat's tha one. I'm gon' buy my momma dat house!" the son says, proudly standing up, pointing in an over exaggerated fashion at the floor plan and looking around the room, nodding at his overly approving brothers and mother.

"Go, baby, go! Go, baby, go! I love you, son," the momma chanted.

I felt like I was in a pep rally, there was so much clapping and chanting going on. Everything the eldest son said was met with approved hoots, hollers, fist pumps, and clapping from the whole family. It was like he just answered a correct question on the *Family Feud* or he was preaching at a southern revival.

"I'm going to ask you a few personal questions so that I can figure out how much of a home you qualify for. Is that okay?" I ask.

"Yeah. You ain't got to worry cause I'm gonna qualify, baby. I got a good job now. I'm making bank!" the son exclaimed. Momma put her hand on her son's shoulder and started to tear up and asked for a Kleenex as tears of pride streamed down her face. The other two younger brothers put their hand reassuringly on their momma's knee.

"What do you make a year at your current job?" I asked. And here is where it got crazy up in my little office.

The son sank back slowly in his chair, looked around the room at his brothers and little nephews as if to say, "Ya'll ready to hear this?" and he beat on his chest twice with his fist and threw up a peace sign high in the air, stood up, and yelled at the top of his lungs, "Eighteen G's! Eighteen G's! Eighteen G's, baby!"

At this proclamation, Momma began to cry again, his little cousins started clapping and yelling, his brothers started chanting, "Ooooh! Ooooh!" and pumping their fists in the air, and the son just continued to hold his peace sign up, relishing the moment.

I was literally trying to hold in hysterical laughter at the crowd of adoring fans in front of me, so I tried to break up the madness by saying, "Okay. That's great! Thank you. Let me see here."

And I looked up what the monthly payments would be and knew I was going to completely have to bust his whole family's bubble, and I didn't want to do it. There was no easy way to say it. I could probably help them find a house but it's not going to be the biggest house we have.

I hesitantly said, "Well, the monthly payments are going to be about $1,700 per month."

And before I could even get it all out, he screamed back at me, still holding his peace sign in the air, "Say WHAT? You trippin' now!"

I jumped so badly that I was afraid my heart stopped at his high-pitched reply. When he said the word "WHAT?" a dog barked in pain next door it was so loud. A collective gasp filled the room as they all look at each other like I was the Antichrist in the middle of a southern Baptist prayer group.

I said, "Unfortunately, that is the truth. The monthly payments per year are a little more than what you are making now." I felt so awful, so I added, "But this is the largest house we sell. We can look at some other ones or I can show you a neighborhood where you can get a house that will fit your needs."

At this, Momma swallowed her pride and began to get angry and started grunting to get up and pull herself out of the chair. "Come on, baby (grunting and heavy breathing), this lady (grunt) don't know what she talking about (another round of heavy breathing). We gonna find a company and a saleslady that wanna sell you a home. She lying. Look at her! You can tell she make a business outta lyin'! Son, you making more money than anybody I know and ain't no house *that* much money a month. I can't believe we even come in here."

I felt like I wanted to cry as she rousted up the three little boys and grabbed the three sons by their shirts and dragged them out of the office mumbling, grumbling, and giving me dirty looks.

As she ambled out of the door barefoot, I kept saying, "I'm sorry," and trying to tell them I could help them find another place. Momma mumbled something about this being worst mistake I'll ever make. The whole ordeal lasted only about five minutes. But it was the most surreal five minutes ever. That was one of my first experiences in new home sales. There are no books that teach you how to handle that situation. Little did I know that there were going to be even more crazy experiences down the road. For the most part, the days are normal. It's the one person out of one hundred who gives me unbelievable stories to tell at the end of the day!

The Model Will Be Closed for Fumigation Sorry for the Inconvenience

Sales

One Sunday afternoon, the parade was dying down a little, but there was a straggler. Here she came, struggling up the monstrous hill that was the walkway into the model home. I secretly took pleasure in watching people struggle up that hill because I had fallen up and down it too many times to count. But that will be another story . . . er, um . . . several stories.

So as I was watching this portly woman in her peacock-themed Sunday dress and hat, I had no idea what was about to happen to me and the model! She walked in the door, bent over trying to catch her breath, put one hand on her knee and one hand was holding her stomach. She held the hand that was on her knee up in the air as if to say, "Hold on a minute, let me get my breath."

We're just standing in the model, with this strange woman bent over, holding her stomach, heaving, and wheezing. I didn't know if I should just let her catch her breath or call 911. Awkward.

Finally, after what seemed like an eternity, I thought we were finally going to exchange names and pleasantries, but that wasn't exactly the case. She managed to wheeze out, while she was moaning and rubbing her stomach, "Uhhhhhhh . . . mmmmm. You gotta baf-room?"

I thought that maybe the walk up had made her sick. But, boy, was I wrong. I pointed to the direction of the "baf-room" and she went inside. And she stayed inside, and stayed inside, and stayed inside. After about thirty minutes, I thought maybe I was going to have to call the coroner. But she emerged from the bathroom with more color in her face and now standing straight up. She simply said, "You have a blessed day," and then she walked out the front door.

I was thinking how weird it was for someone just to come in and use the restroom without looking at the model until, bam! I was knocked over by a smell that could only be defined as corpses in a landfill simmering in rotten milk. I started dry heaving and left the room but the smell had already permeated the whole house! I held my nose as I ran through the model and opened some windows yet somehow could still smell the stench through my mouth.

As I dry heaved again and threw up in my mouth a little, I realized that if anyone came to the model to *really* look at it, that they would think that I did this! So I made a sign, locked up the model, and took a late lunch break.

Drunken Karaoke, Kimchi, and Iced Beer

I always loved to visit my clients after they had closed on their new home and moved in. It was a great feeling to see them situated and so happy. It was during one of these visits that the most hilarious and most uncomfortable experiences I've ever had took place.

I was selling in a local neighborhood and a good friend of mine and local realtor brought in some very sweet clients who were Korean to build a home with me. They brought us the most amazing and delicious food all the time! I was kind of sad when they closed on their home because they were really the nicest people, and now they didn't have a reason to stop by the office anymore with my favorite Korean foods.

So my friend, Christy, the realtor, and I decided we would visit our clients who had just closed on their home a week prior. Christy stopped by my office, we jumped in my car, and headed over to our clients' new home unannounced to bring them a closing gift and to congratulate them officially.

As we drove up, I noticed they were home because the front door was open, but the screen door was shut and I could see the light on in the living room and their cars were in the driveway. Christy and I began to walk up to the front door and as we did, we heard the loudest music blaring from inside the house and then . . . there was a voice. It sounded like someone was wounding a dying old man. There were a lot of "uuuuugggggghhh" and "yaaaaauuuuuggggh" sounds.

Christy and I looked at each other dumbfounded while standing at the screen door on the front porch. I rang the doorbell and instantly a slurred voice yelled at us from inside. No one came to the door. We looked at each other wondering if we should ring again. I rang the doorbell again and the slurred voice yelled at us even louder this time. We were about to turn away and head back to the car when the owner's wife, Ms. Yoon, literally ran to the door which swung open and into me with her full weight nearly knocking me down.

She clamored her way around the door, tripped, and grabbed me, so I was holding up all of her weight. She breathed up into my face and reeked of alcohol! Mrs. Yoon was ripped! Christy looked at me with shock, and I was just standing there holding up Mrs. Yoon who was slurring about how happy she was to see me and that I should come in.

I propped her up against the wall of the front porch and she managed to stay upright. Christy and I realized it was not a good time to visit and told her that we would come back later. Meanwhile, the horrible dying vocal sounds were still streaming out of the house. Mrs. Yoon grabbed Christy's arm and then my arm and yanked us inside and told us that we were going to come inside with her and eat kimchi. She had made it just for us, even though she didn't know we were coming.

As we all staggered into the entryway being dragged by a drunken woman, I realized where the horrible singing was coming from. There was a woman lying on her back on the floor of the living room, holding on her stomach a glass of beer with ice in it, with a microphone propped up to her mouth, staring at the words of a song on the TV, singing Korean karaoke. It was the worst singing I've ever heard. I think she might have been crying too. It must have been a sad song.

Mrs. Yoon introduced her drunken sister to us, which did not stop her from singing or lying on the floor or drinking her iced beer. Christy looked at me with an urgent look that meant, "Let's get out of here!"

I was thinking the same thing and I said, "Mrs. Yoon, we just wanted to drop off your gift and we've got to go."

"No . . . no . . . no . . . you stay and eat Kimchi. I make just for you," Mrs. Yoon said while she handed me and Christy an iced beer each. I turned it down and said I was still on the clock and Christy just held hers uncomfortably.

Next, she handed each of us a plate of kimchi and told us to sit down. We were still listening to the death tones of her sister lying on the floor. I ate a couple of bites of kimchi and told her again that we had to go and thanked her for the hospitality. Christy hadn't uttered a word since we'd been there. She was still just staring at the drunken sister act on the floor.

Of course, Mrs. Yoon still did not want us to leave and was swilling down iced beer by the half glass full. After one big swig, she looked at me and said, "I know you sing, right? I remember you tell me you singer. You sing song before you go. You don't leave until you sing song. I have song for you to sing. Only English song I have. You sing it for me and my sister before you go and we all dance."

Christy grabbed my arm in a death grip and my heart flipped. I just wanted out of there, but she was already cueing up the karaoke machine and her sister was slowly getting up off the floor to dance. Mrs. Yoon smashed a microphone in my face and before I knew it, the song had started. It was Madonna's famed hit, "Like a Virgin."

How was it the *only* English song she had? I'm really going to sing this in front of drunken Korean women? They're going to dance? I was running out of time, I had to make a decision. To sing or not to sing? I wanted to get out of there quickly soooo . . .

"I wandered through the wilderness. Somehow I made it through," I sang as Christy put her head in her hands, resigned to the fact that it would be another excruciating three and half minutes here. She was right. It would get worse. As I continued to sing, Mrs. Yoon and her sister grabbed Christy, they stood her up, all held hands encircling me and staggered around in a ring around the rosies fashion while bumping into me in the middle and stumbling into each other. Christy at this point could no longer hold in her laughter, and she was laughing out loud while being led around in a circle by these two women while I'm singing "Like a Virgin."

Finally, it was over. Everyone clapped and yelled and held up their iced beers. This had been the most fun afternoon of work I had had in months! We gave Mrs. Yoon her gift card and hugged everyone goodbye while they were still drunkenly humming the tune to Madonna's song. As we left, we heard the sister start the song up again and sang it this time in Korean. There was a surreal quality to the air as we left the front door and walked down the driveway to my car. As we sat in the car, we couldn't even look at each other for fear of eruption. We just knew that a legendary moment had just occurred. That was over eight years ago, and Christy and I still laugh about that day every time we see each other. I've never had another experience come close to that.

The lesson to be learned here is to always make an appointment to visit your clients who have just moved in. You never know when someone is going to jam kimchi, iced beer, and a microphone in your face and force you to perform horrible eighties vocals before you can be released. At least know ahead of time if they have any decent English songs you can sing. "Like a Virgin" is so over.

IT'S ALL DOWNHILL FROM HEELS . . .

Years of abuse to my knees and ankles while an athlete in high school and college have created eons of hilarious stories for me. There are very few days in my life since I left college that I haven't turned my ankle or wrenched my knee. It's normal for me to fall at least once a day. Not that I need to add this as a sales tactic to all the latest sales help books, but it seriously works! Turn your ankle, get some empathy, build some rapport, and let them laugh hysterically at their clumsy but loveable sales rep and then your customers buy a home from someone who has provided a one-of-a-kind experience.

It was a bright Texas day in May, and I was feeling great about myself. I had a new white pinstripe suit on with some new platform black heels. (If I could interject ominous, impending doom music here, I would. Heels equal big trouble.)

I was meeting my customers and our construction manager on site at their home. This particular home was being built at the top of a small hill with a very steep slope. I made it up the hill fine and had a great meeting with my customers. They left and I stayed to speak with the construction manager for a while, and then I left to go back to the office. As I walked out of the house, looking fabulous in my white pinstripe suit, holding my clipboard, and maneuvering through the debris on the site to get to my car, I was feeling pretty good about myself. I'm being extra careful because it is a very steep hill with nothing but dirt and rocks on the way down. I make the mistake of looking at my notes on my clipboard as I walk and my heel catches a rock and I turn my ankle. Here's the slow motion play-by-play:

My ankle completely turns and my foot comes unhinged from my leg and makes a sound like a wet two by four breaking in half.

I scream out in pain and launch myself forward and down the hill.

I hit the ground chest and face first, which knocks the breath out of me.

I roll up in a ball because my ankle is radiating pain the likes that I've never felt.

Being that I am now in a ball, I have become more aerodynamic and begin to roll down the hill in the dirt and the rocks in my beautiful new white pinstripe suit.

Since the hill is about a forty degree angle, I finally come to a stop after three and half rolls down the hill.

Grabbing my ankle, I get a chance to really assess my situation and feel the horrible pain from my throbbing foot.

I begin to cry and I'm completely covered in dirt from my triple lutz roll down the hill, so my tears have created mud streams down my face.

Trying to get up, I put a little weight on my foot, hit the ground again, and just wail and cry in the fetal position.

Papers are flying everywhere, I'm covered in dirt with mud streams running down my face, and I'm lying on the ground propping myself up with one elbow wailing in pain.

Two homeowners drive right by me and honk and wave really big as if this is a normal everyday occurrence. "There's that crazy Myka, she's at it again. Honk honey!"

My construction manager runs out and asks what happened. I can't talk because of the pain.

He tried to help me up. He weighs one hundred pounds. I weigh . . . uh . . . more. He pulls me up, we *both* fall down again.

So I crawled to my car and get in and cry a cry of embarrassment and shame for another five minutes and vow to call Jenny Craig.

I drive using my left foot (good foot) on the pedals down to the office, hobble into my office chair and my sales partners begin buzzing around getting ice packs, snacks, water, and cigarettes. You know; everything you'd need to survive an ankle turn.

My sales manager gets wind of the fact that I've been injured on the job. He's a great manager, but since I could probably sue the company, he's not very friendly today.

I tell him what happens, he looks at my ankle and says, "You've got two minutes to figure out if you want to go to the hospital or not." And then he walks off and starts to talk on his cell phone.

I said, "I think I'll be fine but look how swollen it is!"

He comes back over, looks at the swollen purple and green ankle, looks at my good ankle, and says, "I can't tell the difference," and walks off.

This was an obvious jab at my size. He was about ninety-five pounds himself. This was the same manager who told the entire sales team during a sales meeting that our goal for the next week was to spend ten minutes on a treadmill per day; that we were all getting fat. He's sweet.

To cut a long story short, I didn't sue the company, my ankle was only turned, and I recovered. We hired a larger construction manager for my subdivision so he could actually pick me up, the cleaners got the dirt stains out of my beautiful new pinstripe suit, and I *did* call Jenny Craig and went on a diet.

SURPRISE!
I HAVE TWO OTHER KIDS!

My sales partner sold a home to a customer a few years ago, and it seemed like it was going to be an open and close deal, and they would move into their new home and thank us and love us forever! Things started to go horribly wrong at their loan application appointment. The husband was overseas, so they set up a conference call with him, the wife, and the loan officer from our mortgage company. Here's what happened that fateful day:

Our loan officer, we'll call him Jason, sits down with Mrs. Crenshaw. They are connected on a conference call to her husband overseas. About midway through the conversation, Jason asked Mr. Crenshaw about the amount that gets taken out of his check every month for child support. Before Mr. Crenshaw could answer, Mrs. Crenshaw interrupted.

"What child support? There aren't any other kids, or any other marriages. What's he talking about, babe?" she asked.

"Uhh . . . I don't know." Mr. Crenshaw said nervously on the line from across the world.

Being the astute, helpful, and detailed person that he is, Jason proceeded to tell them how much has been taken out each month and for how long. Basically for the last four years, he's been shelling out about $1,400 per month that his wife didn't know about.

"What the heck is going on? Who are you giving child support to? When did you have other kids?" she was yelling over the speaker phone in Jason's office.

After she had finished screaming question after question without giving time for an answer, things got quiet and Mr. Crenshaw answered her.

"That's none of your business! It's my business. Just so you know, I have two other kids from another woman, and I'm not going to stop paying her child support!"

Turns out, a few years after he married Mrs. Crenshaw, he had an affair that lasted quite a while and ended up having a couple of children by her, and she said she'd go public unless he paid her monthly. So he had it taken out of his check directly so that his wife would never even see that money. That is until they bought a house!

Mr. Crenshaw said to Mrs. Crenshaw, "You can stay out of my business and never mention this again and have a beautiful new house, or you can get mad, call a lawyer, get a divorce, and you *won't* get a beautiful new house. So what's it gonna be?"

Here's the part I don't understand . . . Mrs. Crenshaw never shed a tear and sat there for a couple of seconds and said, "You're right, baby. I love you. That's your business. We can move forward," and she nodded her approval to Jason, the loan officer.

Mrs. Crenshaw was okay with everything as long as the amount being taken out didn't interfere with their chances of buying a home. Thankfully, it didn't. I think Jason, the loan officer, was more shocked and upset than Mrs. Crenshaw. She seemed to take a sigh of relief when she knew that she could still get the house!

Remarkably, they stayed together just so they could get the house. They are still together to this day, and no one has ever mentioned that day again. They seem happy, and I guess for them anyway, they have gone back to the "don't ask, don't tell" aspect of their marriage.

THE FORBIDDEN FRUIT

When you're working in new home sales, model home furniture and decorations get used over and over again for years. When one model closes, another model opens up with a lot of the same decorations. It saves the builder money. One Saturday afternoon, there were not many customers in the model, but I was going back and forth talking with a couple of them.

There was a nice old lady in there who wasn't going to buy a home, but she just wanted to look around. The second time I came back to speak with her, she had a handful of something behind her back and a mouthful of food. I usually have some snacks out for people, but this particular day I did not. I just thought she brought something in for herself.

I left to speak with the other clients, came back to her munching on more food, and still holding her hand behind her back. I couldn't figure it out. Finally, when she left, I saw that she had an orange in her hand. I went back through the model and was trying to figure out if I had left some food out or if there was food in the refrigerator that I had forgotten about.

As I was looking around, I noticed that our giant jar of cookies that was on the kitchen counter as decoration was completely empty. I also noticed that a couple of the pieces of waxed fruit on the display chopping block on the kitchen island were gone as well. Turns out, she had eaten about twenty-five, eight-year-old chocolate chip cookies, tried to take a bite out of a fake apple, and left two sets of teeth marks on it, tried to chew up a plastic grape, spit it out and left it chewed up on the counter, and left the model with a fake waxed orange and a can of fake soup. Since then, I always tried to have real food for people. I hope she's okay.

AND THE LORD SPOKE
UNTO MY CUSTOMERS . . .

I sold a home to a very interesting man who happened to be a local minister. We'll call him James. James and I had a very good relationship. My father is a Baptist minister and a Bible professor, so I grew up in church, and I am also a Christian. James and I had some long interesting conversations about growing up in a church and some funny experiences. At times, he would get a little off on a limb and talk about some strange stuff. So when he came in one day with the most outrageous request I've ever heard, I will never forget this as long as I live. Here's how that conversation went:

"Come on in, James. How are you today?" I asked.

"I'm great, thanks, but I need to have a serious talk with you."

This was different. Usually when people said they need to have a serious conversation with me, something was wrong with their home or they were going to cancel their contract. So I steadied myself for the impending bad news.

"Talk to me, James. What's bothering you?" I asked him, looking at him perplexed.

"Well, you know that I talk to the Lord. The Lord has been talking to me about this house and about your company," he says.

I'm trying to figure out if he's kidding or if he's serious at this point. Then he starts to wipe his brow, and I realize that he's completely serious and has put a lot of thought into this.

"God told me that your company has got plenty of money . . . and that you . . . need to give me some of that money. My money. My free stuff. God says that I deserve to have some free stuff," he stated matter-of-factly.

We sat there in awkward silence staring at each other, while I tried to figure out what to say. I had to handle this gently because he was very passionate about what the Lord told him. So after about a minute of staring each other down, I said, "Well, James, you know that I speak to the Lord as well . . . and God told me that you ain't getting jack."

After about five long seconds, we both just stared at each other and then howled with laughter for at least fifteen minutes. The Lord works in mysterious ways and sometimes you can't always get what you want. He didn't get his free stuff.

THE LEGENDARY
JOHNNY ROBINSON

When Johnny Robinson walked through my office door one evening before closing time, I could have never even dreamed of the drama that would soon ensue over the course of a couple of months. Johnny was a very nice-looking black man who definitely had a confident air, swagger, and way too many women in his life!

The night he came in, he had a cute little girl on his arm who didn't say anything. It was so strange. He didn't even introduce her but really seemed to like the fact that she was hanging on to him. He said that he would like to build a house here, he has a good job making plenty of money, and this was the neighborhood he wanted to live in. So we set an appointment to meet the next day.

Before he left, he mentioned something about his girlfriend, Jeanie. So I said, "It's nice to meet you, Jeanie, and I'll see you tomorrow for our meeting, Johnny." He just nodded and swaggered out the door with Jeanie still clinging to his arm and leaning lovingly against him.

Well, that was weird, I thought to myself. The next day, Johnny came in by himself and he didn't even want to talk about the house. He instantly started talking about his girlfriend, Jeanie.

"She ain't my girlfriend you know," he blurted out.

"Excuse me?" I asked.

"Jeanie. She ain't my girlfriend. She thinks she is, but she ain't," he stated.

"Okay," I said, and I didn't really know where to go from there, but before I could even start to talk about the home, he started talking again.

"If anyone comes up here to talk to you about me, you don't know me and never heard of me. I'm not building a house here," he stated.

I was confused and said, "I don't understand. What's going on?"

"There's lots of people who want to get all up in my business, and I just don't want anyone to know what I'm doing," Johnny said.

"I can appreciate that," I said. And that was it. We started talking about the house.

The next day, Jeanie, the girlfriend/not girlfriend came in by herself to talk to me. If you remember, she didn't say a word the first time we met.

"Don't tell Johnny I came out here," she instantly pleaded.

"Ummm . . . okay. Why?" I asked.

"Because . . . I don't want him to get mad at me. Did he say anything about me? Did he say anything about his wife?"

Okay, this was the first time I had heard anything about a wife. I just figured his wife was about to be an ex-wife since he was dating Jeanie. "No and no. Why?" I asked again. I was really getting interested at this point.

"Because he has a wife who doesn't know about me and doesn't know that we're building a house together. She's crazy and he wants to leave her. He doesn't let her leave the house, so I don't think that she'll find out," she said matter-of-factly.

Now this was getting good. "He doesn't let her leave the house?" I asked. What do you mean?"

"She's really stupid, and he doesn't want her to get out of the house and embarrass him, so he took her car away and he calls her all the time to make sure she's home. Sometimes, he leaves her tied to the bed so she can't go nowhere. He wants to get away from her."

I couldn't believe she was even saying this. Doesn't she know that sounds like he's crazy? And she's crazy? I tried to think how I could make this conversation a little saner. So I started talking in legal terms.

"His wife will have to sign for the house when he signs the closing documents. The state of Texas says that she'll own half if she's still his wife then."

"Just don't tell your company that he's married so she doesn't have to sign the papers," she said, starting to sound a little desperate and scared.

"I don't feel really comfortable with this anymore. I'm sorry, Jeanie, I'll have to talk about these details with Johnny," I said.

She started crying and said, "Oh god, please don't tell him I was here."

My heart went out to her, and I told her I wouldn't tell him.

The next day, I saw Johnny pull up to the model, and I watched him go around to the passenger side of the car and open the door for a girl who definitely wasn't Jeanie. A beautiful tall Asian woman stepped out of the car and gave Johnny a kiss, and he kissed her back.

What the crap is going on here? I was thinking to myself. *This* has *to be his wife*. But I've learned never to assume the other woman is the wife.

When they walked in the door, I greeted Johnny and introduced myself mainly because I was so curious to find out who the heck the new girl was.

"I'm Lisa," she said. "I'm Johnny's fiancé."

Now imagine me with a horrific, shocked look on my face, staring at Lisa, then Johnny, then Lisa, then Johnny. I have a problem with not being able to control the looks on my face. It gets me in trouble a lot.

Lisa says to Johnny in a playful tone, "Didn't you tell her about me?"

"Not yet, baby," he said and gave her a doting kiss.

I started looking around for a hidden video camera. This had to be a joke. So I just had a nice conversation with them for a while, and then they left, and I was still in shock. *What else is going to happen?* I thought to myself.

Less than thirty minutes later, a really nicely dressed woman pulled up and walked into the model. She was very quiet and demure, and she said, "My name is Linda Robinson, Johnny Robinson's wife."

My jaw dropped, and I couldn't hide my shock anymore and frankly didn't want anymore to do with this. Suddenly, I felt like I was the bad person for catering to this crazy person named Johnny Robinson.

I said, "It's nice to meet you, Linda." We had a nice conversation in which she told me that she knew that he had a girlfriend and a fiancé and that he was about to leave both of them and they were going to be able to start over and live in the new house together. She said that she loved him and didn't want to give up on him. Of course, I didn't tell her that he was just here with his fiancé, Lisa, and they were putting on a pretty good public display.

The next time Johnny came in to visit with me, I told him how uncomfortable I was trying to hide all of this from all of the women in his life. He said to just not talk about it with any of them and that he was going to break up with his girlfriend Jeanie and get a divorce from his wife and marry Lisa, the fiancé.

I told him that unless he was divorced before the house was done, his wife will have to sign for the house. He insisted that he would "take care of everything."

In the next month, there wasn't a day that went by that I didn't get a visit from one of Johnny's women. It became a running joke and much like a daily soap opera. Here's where the story gets hilarious and comes to a ridiculous end.

I warned the loan officer about Johnny's situation, and so she knew that it was a toss-up whom he would bring to his loan application appointment. He ended up bringing his fiancé, Lisa.

The loan officer had to ask him about his wife, because she had to sign the application papers too. At that point, things spun totally out of control for the legendary Johnny Robinson!

At the mention of a wife, Lisa, the fiancé, came completely undone and started screaming at him in the office and cussing at him with every bad word you can imagine. She had no idea he was married. So they were screaming and cussing at each other in the office and you could hear it throughout the building because it was so loud. The loan officer, Vicky, could only sit there and watch. She was trying to calm them down and interject, but it was fruitless.

As if things couldn't get worse, they did! In the middle of the fight between Johnny and Lisa, Jeannie, his girlfriend, who had been driving around looking for Johnny, found his car and marched herself right in, heard the fight and busted the door open to Vicky's office with a swift, karate-style kick and started yelling at Johnny too!

Johnny had lightning fast reactions and closed the office door on Jeanie so fast that it knocked her across the hall and into the wall with a thud! Jeannie came back with a vengeance trying to bust through the door. Johnny was pushing it closed with all his might with his back against it while he was pleading with Lisa to forgive him.

Well, now Lisa was asking who *this* girl was banging on the door to get in and Vicky, the loan officer, just laid her head down on her desk and gave up. Finally, they were escorted out of the building, Jeanie, kicking and screaming, Lisa, crying and basically running to get away from Johnny, and Johnny looking like a lost puppy dog with no women left.

Johnny never bought a house, his girlfriend Jeanie came back to him because she's crazy. His wife is still sitting at home waiting for him to come back to her, and Lisa is hopefully long gone.

Johnny's house was halfway built when I had to cancel the deal and I sold it to a wonderful couple who are drama-free. No one to this day has beat Johnny with the amount of drama that he brought into my life. That is why he will forever be referred to as "The Legendary Johnny Robinson." I often tune into Jerry Springer for the sole reason of expecting to see him as the main guest one day with multiple women taking swings at him.

SOME SCABS
JUST DON'T HEAL

If you've been in sales long enough or worked with the public long enough, you can spot *crazy* from a mile away. When this particular woman walked in the door, *crazy* was so rampant through her veins that I could smell it even before she turned the corner into the subdivision. Let's take a moment to give you a good visual of this woman.

She had the body and posture of a concentration camp victim. She was basically skin and bones, sallow with bright orange hair that looked like it hadn't seen a brush or shampoo for that matter in months. She was wearing a plain green T-shirt and gray sweatpants. As she walked in the door, I noticed that her right hand was busy scratching at something on her left arm.

She walked right past me and sat down in my office. So I thought, *Okay, I guess we'll just sit down and talk first.* So I walked into my office, sat down, and said, "How can I help you t-t-t-to-d-d-d-ay?" I could barely get the words out before I noticed that her entire arms were covered in scabs, her face, her scalp and I'm sure other places that I'm so fortunate I couldn't see. I could tell she was nervous because she was busily picking the bleeding scab on one of her arms while I was busily holding down lunch vomit.

She then started a legendary rant. "I've got a lot of money and I live in a huge house right now, but my husband is leaving me so I need to move into something different. I have two other kids, they're not here right now, but they're going to be coming with me, well, not really coming with me, they're with my husband, he's an NBA basketball star, and he's really good and really rich, and the kids are going to be staying with him and coming to visit me. But only with supervised visits, but that's okay with me.

I really like my house now but I just need to get my own place. I don't have a job or anything right now, but I will have one really soon. I've been talking with a lot of people, and I think I'll be making a lot of money really soon, you know because my husband made all the money before and I don't know how to be poor. I like nice stuff and I'm really good at a lot of stuff like scrapbooking, cleaning, cooking, and I could probably counsel people because all my friends call me when they have a problem and I always help them fix their problems. Yeah! That's what I'll do; I'll just listen to other people's problems and help them. Those people make a lot of money, right? So do you have a house I can buy?" she rambled.

Now . . . she barely took a breath during this entire monologue and there was so much more that she talked about, I just can't remember everything. As if the incoherent ramblings of this woman weren't enough, the entire time she was talking, she wasn't even looking at me; she was pulling off every scab on her arm and gently placing them on my desk. There were probably twenty-three different scabs lying on my desk. I have a weak stomach, so I was stifling a severe barf, and I just wanted to run out of there and never come back. I knew I was going to have to clean that up, and I have never seen anything more disgusting.

She was looking at them like they were her precious babies, like Gollum from the *Lord of the Rings* movies fame would look at his precious ring.

She was positioning them in designs. First a straight line, then a circle, then an abstract artwork. At first I truly believed that she would scoop them up in her hand, cuddle them, and take them home to tuck them in for bed before making them a nice hot cup of cocoa. Unfortunately, she left them on my desk for me to love and care for later.

I did not show her any homes, mainly because I was afraid that I would throw up, but also because she didn't have a job or income! I made a couple of calls to a few of my friends in real estate and explained what had happened, and they knew exactly who I was talking about. Turns out, she's has been deemed legally incompetent and is a habitual model shopper and contract writer. It also turns out that she has a terrific heroin problem, thus the skin malfunctions.

If you're wondering, I called a professional cleaning team to completely fumigate and clean my office. It was really hard to come back with the image of those scabs lying on my desk. Sometimes, I lay awake at night in a cold sweat, gripping the sides of the bed with visions of flaky things rolling through my head. I guess you could say I have post-traumatic stress disorder from that particular interaction. I still hear stories that she has continued to try to buy homes from other salespeople. I think if she happens to walk into my office again, I will have a post-traumatic stress induced flashback, dry heave, and run out the back door never to return. To this day, if anyone walks in with a visible scab, I get an uncontrollable head twitch.

COTTON CANDY

Some buyers are not informed about the home construction process. I know, it's impossible to believe, but it's entirely true. This is a short and sweet story about a single young man who came to visit me about buying a home. He had purchased a home before, and one might think that maybe he had learned something through that purchase. But obviously, we're giving way too much credit where there is no credit due. He was nice enough, but there was a little something off that I could never put my finger on.

As we looked for homes, we got into a discussion about the construction workers in our homes. Here is how that conversation went:

"You know, this company is very proud of the construction teams that represent us. We take a lot of pride in our work and welcome you out to the job site anytime to see our progress and to help you better understand the construction process," I said, feeling pretty good about being able to sell him a home at this point.

"I hope you're right because I had a terrible experience with the last house that we had built," he said with a deeply perplexed look on his face. I could tell he was very troubled about this experience.

"What happened, if you don't mind me asking?" I asked.

My philosophy is to let them air out their grievances and then tell them how we can be different and help them feel better about it.

"These dudes who worked on my house were so messy! They left all kinds of crap behind. The worst was that they left this horrible cotton candy-looking stuff all in the attic. I can't even get around in there there's so much cotton candy!" he said, obviously very upset.

"It's so itchy! I couldn't stop scratching when I went up there. Ya'll won't leave any cotton candy behind in this house, will you? Because if you do, I'm not buying here. That stuff is so gross!"

I wanted to die laughing so bad, but I didn't want to make him feel dumb from the question I was about to ask.

"Do you know what insulation looks like?" I asked.

"No. What's insulation?" he said.

I explained to the best of my ability what it was and why he needed it, but he didn't want any more cotton candy, so he left to find a builder that doesn't use cotton candy. Good luck!

Nothing

a Few Nails Can't Fix

I was selling in a high-end neighborhood where the buyers were pretty finicky, picky, and grumpy. They've been around the block before and basically watched with eagle eyes, every part of the construction process. One of those customers was a lieutenant colonel who was very highly esteemed in the army. The first day he came in to visit me, he had 8x10 full color photos of all the options and upgrades that he would like in his home. They were laminated, categorized, and alphabetized. I knew that this was going to be a long six-month build process.

His daily routine was to come to the home being built after work and watch the workers work with his hands on his hips and make sure that no one made any mistakes. Those poor little workers were so scared every day. They tried to work fast so that they could be done before he had a chance to come by. This particular gentleman wanted to keep every single cedar tree on his property that was possible. He watched anyone working close to the trees to make sure that they didn't damage them.

If you live in Texas, you know that we regard cedar trees like we regard weeds. They choke out and kill all the beautiful oak trees and they attract ticks. I know, gross. I told the lieutenant colonel all of these things, but he loved those ugly trees.

One day, he came in all in a huff and couldn't even speak. He finally got a hold of himself and started to laugh hysterically. I kept asking what was wrong, but he couldn't even speak. He just said, "Come with me. You have to see this."

I couldn't even imagine what had his emotions rolling up and down so much. So when we got to his house, we walked over to a clump of trees and he said, "Look at that."

It was a cedar tree, but I couldn't tell what the big deal was. He said, "Look closer."

The workers had accidently knocked over one of his big cedar trees and completely chopped it in half. They were so scared of him that they had put the tree back together and nailed it back on with a nail gun so that he wouldn't notice. There were probably a hundred nails holding this tree together. Only thing is that the nails were starting to give way and it was leaning sickly to one side. I just had to start laughing. I had to give the construction guys plus points for thinking outside the box though. They really nailed that one.

Russian Mail-Order Bride, Anyone? She's Worth Fifteen Million!

This is one of the most unbelievable stories that I have to tell. I've never had anyone rival the likes of a girl named Laura. She's only the fourth person that I've ever talked to who has said they have actually won millions from a lawsuit.

Laura was a sweet twenty-three-year-old girl with the worst dental hygiene and least amount of teeth for someone so young whom I've ever seen in my whole life. And I've traveled to many other southern states, so that's saying a lot! I hate to be mean, but I really need to paint the picture for you because it's a vital part of the story.

Laura came to visit with me one afternoon with her new fiancé. She was a very happy girl, which was sort of unnerving considering the random and protruding teeth problem. She was normal-looking enough but obviously pregnant. Immediately she took to me, telling me her name and that she and her fiancé were expecting a baby girl.

She loved my name and asked if it would be okay if they used it. I thought that was a little strange after our first meeting, but okay. So we got past the pleasantries and we sat down in my office for the most revealing and unbelievable story I've ever heard. Here are all of the things that I was told during this initial meeting:

1. I was in a car wreck where I was almost killed last year.
2. In that car wreck, I hit the steering wheel and lost all of my teeth. (Don't feel sorry for her just yet.)
3. I was pregnant during that car wreck and lost the baby.
4. Because of how injured I was, I was awarded $15 million in a court case.
5. I'm about to receive nine million of those dollars in the next month.
6. I have two other children from another marriage.
7. My ex-husband stole my other two children, and I don't know where they are. We're currently hunting him down so I can get my children back.

8. I almost found them when I went to visit his parent's house in Alabama and I accidentally lost control of my car and rammed it through his house. During that incident, he got away and took the kids with him, and I haven't seen him since.

9. I'm just lucky to be here because my mom is in the Russian Mafia. She's wanted in the United States for money laundering.

10. My mom wanted me to have a better life than she could provide for me in Russia, so she sold me as a Russian mail-order bride to an American business man when I was sixteen.

11. I stayed married to him until I was nineteen. He was really nice and set me up with some money.

12. Then I met my ex-husband and we had two kids together. He went crazy and took my kids away from me.

13. We want to buy two houses from you. One for me and my fiancé and one for my mom to live in when she comes down from Russia. (Yes. The one who is wanted in the United States for Russian Mafia money laundering.)

14. I hope that my current baby is okay, because I fell on my stomach at the air show.

15. Oh, these bruises on my upper arm? (Accusing glance at fiancé) I fell on a boat dock.

After all that, it was such an unbelievable story that I had to believe it. Who could make anything like that up?

So we wrote up two contracts for two houses that she was going to buy from me. In the next weeks, she brought me bank account information that showed she was ready for the $9 million to go into it with routing information from the bank to our company for the cost of the home. Everything, as crazy as it sounds, seemed like it was falling into place, and it was one of the easiest sales I've ever made, although easy sales tend to be too good to be true. A little foreshadowing, maybe?

The closing date came and went for Miss Laura and she came in and said that her lawyer assured her that the money would come in. It was just caught up in the system. So we set another close date. That close date came and went.

Then she gave birth to a new baby girl. I got a phone call one afternoon and a breathless Laura was on the phone and she wasn't making any sense. She sounded confused. Breathlessly she said, "I had the baby!"

I said, "Great! When did you have it?"

"About fifteen minutes ago. They're wheeling me back into my room," she managed to wheeze out.

"What? What are you doing calling me? You need to rest!" I said. I couldn't believe what I was hearing, but I actually heard the doctors and nurses talking to her as she was talking to me on the phone.

"I snuck my phone into the labor room so I could call you as soon as I had her. I named her after you. I named her Myka," she said proudly.

I was really starting to feel strange. I didn't want to encourage this strange and unnatural relationship anymore. I barely knew this person, and she's calling me while she's being wheeled back into her room after childbirth and naming her daughter after me? Oh god! This is not happening!

I didn't know what to say except "Wow. Thank you. Congratulations. You need to rest. I'll talk to you later."

She had this desperation in her voice and said, "Okay. Will you call me later?"

Whoa. This is really headed down the wrong way. "You just rest, okay?" I said.

After that, I didn't hear from her for about two weeks, and I had to cancel her sales contracts because she wouldn't answer any of my calls or any of the calls from the company I was working for as well.

One night, I was working late at the office and got a strange call from a man who said he was a lawyer who was representing Laura in a current custody hearing. I checked his credentials and looked up his company on the Internet, and he was on the up-and-up. Unbelievably, here is what he told me!

1. She was never in any car wreck.
2. Since there was no car wreck, there was no loss of teeth. I'll never know how she just ended up with four rotten teeth at such a young age.
3. Again, since there was no car wreck, there was no baby who was lost. However, she had been pregnant before and tried to lose it herself by throwing herself downstairs and falling.
4. There is no $15 million that will be awarded to her. In fact, there is a court case open right now, but it's against her.
5. There was no $9 million that was going to be immediately awarded to her.
6. She doesn't have two other children; she has five!
7. Her ex-husband didn't take her children from her; a court named her an indecent parent and awarded the kids to the father.
8. When she visited her ex-husband's house in Alabama, she didn't accidentally lose control of her car. She ran it through the living room, backed out, and got away from the police.
9. Her mom is not in the Russian Mafia. She's never even been to Russia or of Russian descent. Her mom is from Alabama and has never been out of the state.
10. Obviously, if the above is true then she was not a mail-order bride. In fact, Laura was born and raised in Alabama.
11. She's only been married once. The older businessman is a complete figment of her imagination.
12. Again, her ex-husband took her kids away from her for being an indecent parent, and a court of law found her legally incompetent.

13. Obviously, she did not buy a house from me. Turns out, she does not have a dollar to her name. She attached herself to her newest fiancé who does not know her past.
14. She *did* fall on her stomach at the air show, but she had a history of trying to lose her babies, purposefully.
15. The bruises on her arm were self-inflicted. Since she was sixteen, she's always thrown herself downstairs, fallen down, and twisted her arms to make bruises and blames other people for the attention.

You can imagine my shock and horror. I was so mad at myself for believing all of those stories. I felt like the biggest idiot! It was all so crazy that I didn't think anyone could make up anything as unreal as that.

To top all of this off, the reason that the lawyer called me is because Laura had submitted into evidence a letter "from me" stating that I was Laura's employer. It said that Laura had been cleaning my house for a year and that I was paying her cash and that was how she was going to support her new baby. The lawyer was trying to subpoena me to court to prove that Laura had a job, but I shot that lie down real quick. That's when he started to ask me questions and let me know the real truth.

I never heard from Laura again, but I assume her life is not what she imagined it would be. I wish her the best, but I'll never be able to forgive myself for being that gullible. I have never since met anyone who was as sincerely and believably crazy as Laura. One thing I never understood was that if I was going to make up a bunch of crap about myself, I'd make it really good! Not a Russian mail-order bride! What? Come on!

AND BARKLAND
WAS HIS NAME-O!

One of the nicest men I had ever met was going to build a home with me. He had a beautiful wife and the cutest little dog ever. He had patiently waited about a year for some new lots to come open, and he would get the first pick of the lots when they opened. During that year, we had become good friends and were ready to get started on his new home when the time came. He was also waiting on a new plan that I had told him we were going to unveil. It was a huge single-story plan, and it was exactly everything that he had ever dreamed of. He was so excited. I was excited too because this was a great plan. I was so emotional about it that as soon as I heard it was available, I called him. Big mistake!

I was very proud of what I was selling and the marketing department had really thought of some great names that were Texas-themed names for all the other plans. So I was expecting a really awesome name for an awesome new plan. They called me and told me that the name of the beautiful new plan was . . . (insert the drumroll here) The Barkland. What? That is the dumbest name I've ever heard! It has nothing to do with Texas! Who was the marketing genius who thought of that? I was actually embarrassed to tell my customer that his dream home was named the Barkland. Here is how that conversation went:

"Mr. Collins! I'm so glad you could come in to see the new plan. I was so excited to call you about it being released to us," I said when he walked excitedly into my office.

"Thank you for calling me. We've only been waiting for this day for a year! Well, let's see it," he said.

"Okay, but I have to tell you something first. I've been sitting here trying to figure out why they named this plan what they did. It is the worst name I've ever heard for a house or for anything for that matter! I'm going to have to have a serious talk with our marketing team. They really screwed this one up." I snorted and laughed.

"Oh my gosh! I can't even imagine. What did they name it?" he said.

"The Barkland!" I said in a mocking singsong voice. I instantly noticed a change on his face, so I thought he was just sharing my disdain for the name as well. "I know, right? It's horrible! Barkland. Barkland. No matter how you say it, it's stupid."

I laughed and realized that I was the only one laughing. He had a majorly hacked off look on his face. I said, "What is it? What's wrong?"

"Barkland is my middle name. Barkland was my father's name, my grandfather's name and his father's name. My dog's name is Barkland as well," he said.

I paused for a second and because we had a great relationship and had known each other for so long, I thought he was kidding with me. So I said, "Ha, ha!" pointing at him, "Good one! Well, I guess this is the perfect house for you. Barkland! If that *is* your real name!" I laughed, thinking he was kidding. Again, I was the only one laughing and just awkwardly ended my laugh with an, "Ahhh."

"I think we're done here. I'm not going to build a home with someone who can be so insensitive. Thank you for making fun of my heritage. Have a nice day," he said sarcastically and got up and started for the door.

Being as quick on the draw as I am (yeah right), I started to apologize to him. It took me a while to realize that he was serious and I had really hurt his feelings. I never heard from him again and I sent cards and left e-mails and phone messages. I, making fun of his name, was enough for him to not want to build a home with me. What are the flipping odds of his having the same stupid name as our new home? I still think it's a stupid name, but if I'd have known, I could've at least lied about it!

A Priest, a Nun, and a Realtor Walk into a Model Home . . .

Growing up as a preacher's daughter has taught me to appreciate all aspects of religious beliefs. I went to all different kinds of churches to experience everything. In my teens, I'd go to the local Catholic church with a friend of mine because if you went to the afternoon session, the priest had already had two services of wine partaking (which he drank randomly during his message), and he would ramble on and on, getting more inebriated by the second. This was fun for me because I don't think my dad or my mom has ever had a sip of alcohol. But a drunken priest was too good to pass up.

A man walked into our office very recently, and he had two women with him. He was normal-looking enough and just as nice as he could be. It was the turn of my partner, John, to take a customer; so he began to talk with them. We had a very laid-back and friendly office; and we often walked into each other's office and asked the customers what they were buying, what they loved about the house, and a little bit about themselves.

So I sauntered over to John's side of the office and noticed that the door was shut. I tried to open it, and it was locked, so if you remember, I'm really quick witted, so I start to knock on the door, smiling stupidly, waiting to get in to talk to our newest neighbors in the community. John gives me a "No, not now!" look and continues to talk with them and ignores me standing there, smiling stupidly like a kid waiting for a candy store to open.

Now I'm totally curious about what's going on because they are talking in hushed tones and haven't come out of the office for two hours. I hear them open the door to leave, so I run out to tell them goodbye and thank you for coming in today. I'm really waiting to get the scoop from John. When they walked out the door, John looked at me like, "You're never going to believe this!"

Knowing there was a good, juicy story here, I asked, "What's the scoop?"

"Mr. Langford is a priest. The smaller woman is a nun. The larger woman is their realtor. The priest is buying a home here. The nun is going to live there too. He doesn't want the church to know that he's buying a house. He also doesn't want the church to know that one of their nuns is going to live with him. He made me swear that I wouldn't tell anyone that he had been here. I'm not even supposed to tell you!"

I started thinking about what I knew about Catholic priests, and I remembered that some take a vow of poverty. The church provides them with shelter and the necessities of life and a small salary. They aren't supposed to own property. Somehow, he has $150,000 in the bank, but he doesn't want to use it. He wants to get a loan but doesn't want anyone to call the church to verify how much money he makes. He took a vow of celibacy, yet he is going to live in sin with his nun!

Man, this is good! I thought. So as we begin building this home for a *not so godly* man of God, I began to get to know them a little more. One day, John was off, and all three of them came in to sign some papers. They couldn't believe that John wasn't there and would not let me help them at all. They were calling John over and over trying to get him on the phone to come in on his day off to help them sign his papers. John finally convinced them that it would be fine to let me help them and assured them that I didn't know anything.

So they timidly entered my office. The priest was a portly man who took up the whole chair; his realtor refused to sit because she took her role as secret keeper to the most dramatic flair possible and wanted to get out of my office as soon as the pen left the paper. The nun, who was as plain as they come, was eager to get started and sitting on the edge of her seat.

I've always tried to find common ground with people to be able to build rapport. Now remember, that I am very quick witted and think things out to make sure that it's the right thing to say (this is sarcasm).

So in order to break the silence and build some crucial rapport here, I say, "My dad's a preacher and my favorite church to go to when I was a kid was the Catholic Church at the third service because the priest was drunk by then and the sermon was always a lot more interesting."

Awkward glances around the room were being shared by everyone in front of me. The nun interjects and says, "Why do you say that? What do you know about him?" she said pointing to her priest-boyfriend.

Dang it! I thought to myself. *Way to go, Myka. How are you going to get out of this one?* So I said, "I can spot a man of the cloth from a mile away. I grew up a preacher's daughter, remember?"

Unfortunately, this did not help me build rapport and they didn't buy my excuse. The anxiety in the room was growing as everyone started asking me what I knew. Oh my god! It was the inquisition!

Finally, I just said, "Guys, don't worry. The only thing I know is that you are a priest. Really. But now I'm *really* interested! Are you in the witness protection program?" I laughed.

They finally laughed and the priest and I shared some knowledge of the Bible, but we didn't speak about that pesky *adultery* or *celibacy* thing. We finished his home for him and his nun-girlfriend came out every day to pray as she walked through the trees of the backyard.

But in the end, karma had other plans in mind for the priest and the nun. They could not get mortgage approval because every mortgage company had to verify his income with the church, and of course, the church could not know about this adulterous new living situation! So after going through several mortgage companies that said they couldn't help him, he finally went back to the boring church parsonage, and I guess he and the nun had to find other places to meet each other and live in utter sin. John and I sighed a sigh of relief. We felt kind of dirty by association for helping a priest do something so horribly sinful!

THE NEAR DEATH
OF A SALESWOMAN

After I had my precious daughter, I seemed to put on a few extra pounds that were nagging at me every time I looked in the mirror. So I decided to go visit the local "fat doctor" (a doctor who prescribes medication to lose weight for lazy people who don't want to exercise) to get a dose of metabolism. It's basically legalized speed. I had been taking these for a while, feeling great, and had lost about ten pounds already. I was, however, feeling increasingly anxious and had felt my heart do some very strange things. I shrugged it off as my boosted metabolism jumpstarting my heart. (I know, it sounds stupid now that I just said it.) All of this to preface the day that I almost died and the not-so-caring realtor who was convinced I was fine. She's *not* a doctor, I might add.

Whether it's global warming, depleted ozone, or just Texas, it was hot in the summer of 2009. We had two straight months with temperatures over the one hundred degree point. With times as rough in the new homes industry as they have been, builders were cutting corners everywhere they could. One of those was not to run the air conditioners in the homes that were currently available (which actually detracted to the sale because people didn't even want to go inside these houses that were hotter inside than it was outside!).

So when a realtor whom I have known a while drove up with customers following her, it was a bittersweet feeling. I wanted to sell a home, but I did not want to leave the air-conditioned office. So I jumped into the car with her (let's say her name was Claire). Claire and I exchanged pleasantries and we set up a plan to see about four different homes that were available.

As Claire and I got out of the car, something started to not feel right with me. I introduced myself to the customers and we walked up to the house. As I was putting the key in the door, I felt my heart do something strange and I again brushed it aside as boosted metabolism.

We walked inside of the three-thousand-square-foot baker's oven where it was one hundred degrees downstairs, and as we were heading upstairs the heat was like a wall hitting us. Everyone was bent over and hurrying through the house to see it as fast as possible in order to get out as fast as possible.

By the time I made it up the stairs, everything started to tunnel out on me. My hands started to tingle, I was light-headed, I couldn't see well, and my heart was racing as beads of sweat ran down my face. I turned to Claire and said, "There's something really wrong with me. I don't feel right."

She said, "It's just hot in here. We need to get outside and you'll feel better."

So I carefully walked down the stairs afraid that I was going to pass out any minute. I walked outside and sat down in Claire's car while she remained outside talking to her clients. I leaned the seat down, and I knew that I was dying at that point. I've never felt anything like what I felt that day.

As I lay back, everything turned black on me and I passed out for a few moments. When I came to, I called my husband, who is a firefighter and an emergency medical technician, and told him what I was feeling. I was scared to death, crying, sweating, could barely see, and could barely form words.

My husband said, "You need to get back to the office and relax. If you still feel the same, call someone."

I told him, "I think this is really serious. I'm with a realtor, and I've got to get to a hospital."

He could hear how scared I was and said, "Well, tell Claire to take you back to the office and see how you feel after you've sat in the air conditioning for a while."

So here's where things get ridiculous. I'll tell it word for word as it happened. I really want you to feel like you were there.

"Claire," I said, panting her name out as I leaned back in her car seat, fanning my face that was milky white and covered in sweat. "Something is wrong. I need you to take me back to the office," I said with my eyes closed because for some reason I couldn't see very well and it scared me to open my eyes.

"Oh, Myka, you'll be fine. You're just hot. I feel like I'm going to die right now too. Now, where is the other home that you're going to show us today?" she asked as if she didn't see the disgusting sweaty dying sales person in the passenger seat.

"I'm serious, Claire. I have never felt like this before and I need to go back to the office," I said, barely getting the sentence out because I was drifting in and out of consciousness. At this point, I was completely laid down in her car, I was shaking uncontrollably, sweating profusely, couldn't open my eyes, and could barely put words together.

"So is it up here on the same street or do I need to take a right turn? What's the price on this next house anyway?" she asked.

I couldn't believe this! Could someone be this cold hearted or desperate to get a sale? I started to really cry because I knew I was probably going to die in Claire's car and I wouldn't ever get the chance or the strength to strangle her to death.

I mustered all of my strength and yelled, "Claire! Take me back to the office! I am dying, and I need an ambulance."

"Okay, but I still think you're just hot. Let me tell my customers what we're going to do. They're going to be mad that they have to follow me back to the office only to backtrack to this next house," she stated, obviously irritated, while she was rolling down the window.

"Hey, guys, Myka is sick, so I'm going to drop her off at the office real quick. Follow me and then we'll go look at that other house. Myka?" She looked at me and asked me again, "Where is the next house?"

"D_ _ _ _ _t, Claire! Take me back to the office!" I was sobbing uncontrollably because I was scared.

"Okay. Let's go," she said.

Finally! I thought to myself. I was fanning myself with the only thing that I had, and that was the list of available homes that I had brought with me to make sure we were going to the right houses. We finally made it to the model, and Claire said . . . oh, you'll never believe this:

"Is it okay if I drop you off at the corner? I want to make sure my customers don't get mad about backtracking," she said.

I was just so glad to be at the model home that I didn't care where she dropped me off. However, I wasn't sure how I was going to get out of the car or walk or more than likely crawl back into my office. It literally took me two minutes to lift myself up out of the car without passing out. Every time I moved, everything went black again.

During these two minutes, I was fanning myself with the available homes list, and that was keeping me from completely passing out from the heat. Claire was sighing with frustration at how long it was taking me to get out of the car, and then in a final act of unbelievable uncaring, she said, "Oh, and, Myka? I'm going to need that available homes sheet you're using."

It was at that moment that I vowed to punch Claire square in the face if I ever lived past this day. So I handed her my only lifeline, my fan, and shakily stood on the street corner with my eyes barely open. She closed the door for me and sped away making sure that she didn't see that I made it to the front door okay. I was talking to myself and trying to put one foot in front of the other. I knew that if I went down on my knees, I'd never get up, and I wanted to live to see me put the hurt on Claire!

As I walked to the front door, I got out my cell phone and told my construction manager to come over here, that I was sick and needed help. He was there in less than a minute. Finally, someone who cares! I sat in my office for a while, trying to get a grip on reality, but it was getting worse. My construction manager called the ambulance.

When the emergency crew got there, I was still on the edge. They took my vitals, and I knew I was in trouble when one of the technicians said, "Holy crap! Look at this!" My heart rate was 214 beats per minute with so many irregular beats that they couldn't believe it. They immediately strapped me to the gurney and put me in the ambulance.

While I was in the ambulance, one of the firefighters said, "Now don't be scared, but this is usually fatal if we can't get your heart rate down. You're about to have heart failure."

Did he just say, "Don't be scared, but this is usually fatal"? I asked myself. So I just started to pray. I made promises to God that I still keep today and will always keep and strangely enough, I was calmed by my prayer and my heart rate started to drop. I wasn't afraid; I knew that whatever happened, I would be okay. I knew where I was going.

Even with two paramedics standing in front of me warming up the paddles and one with an epinephrine shot waiting for the moment when my heart stopped, I felt nothing but calm. Just as they were about to put the paddles to my chest to jumpstart my heart when it failed, my heart rate began to drop to normal. If you don't believe, there *is* power in prayer, in faith, and in God. The paramedic said, "Would you look at that? It's almost instantly back to normal! I've never seen that."

Meanwhile, back at the model . . . Claire had come back with her customers and walked right past the ambulance and up to the front door where one of my coworkers was standing, and she said, "Is that Myka in there?"

"Yes," he said in a very concerned voice. "It's pretty serious."

"Oh my god!" she said, totally ticked off. "Does this mean that the model will be closed for the rest of the day and no one will be here to help me?"

My coworker couldn't believe what he just heard and in an incredulous tone said, "Yes. That's what that means," and walked off.

Obviously, I didn't die. I lived to write this book. It turns out that the diet pills had built up in my system and had caused enough heart damage that I was really in trouble. I stayed at the hospital until my heart rate went down, but I was left with an irregular heartbeat that they said would not kill me but was not great either.

I'm fine and have not had another near-death experience since that day. I have not seen Claire since that day either, and I have thought long and hard about what I would say to her and I still don't have it planned out, but I think it will start with a punch to the face, then I'll drop her off on a street corner somewhere far, far way and ask her if this will be okay for her to walk home from here. Is that wrong?

ANYONE CAN SPEAK A FOREIGN LANGUAGE! JUST . . . SPEAK . . . SLOWLY . . . AND . . . LOUDLY!

Every once in a while, you are introduced to a couple who you know should definitely not be together. You know, like Britney and Kevin, Michael Jackson and Lisa Marie Presley, and the couple who came to see me one bright spring day. Their names were Mr. and Mrs. Lester. What I notice immediately is that Mr. Lester is a nice looking Hispanic gentleman who is in a wheelchair and his wife is a very petite Asian woman. What I can also notice immediately is a fog of hatred and disdain between them that I could cut with a knife. As Mrs. Lester wheeled her husband in the front door, I had no idea how uncomfortable it was about to become.

On this day, I tried the usual, "How are you today? How are you enjoying this beautiful weather we're having? What were you hoping to find today?" Here are the answers that I received to those questions:

"How are you today?" I asked.

Mr. and Mrs. Lester look at each other with nasty looks as if to say, "Are *you* going to answer her or what?" But Mr. Lester finally answers as if it is painful to release the air out of his lungs and across his lips. He says, "Fine," and continues to stare at the ground.

"How are you enjoying this beautiful weather?" I ask them.

As if they haven't even had a chance to look outside and notice that it's a gorgeous day, they both look out the window and then Mrs. Lester makes a grunting sound and shrugs her shoulders. Mr. Lester just looks back down at the ground.

Well, this is going well! Let's just get to business then. Small talk is not working today.

"What were you hoping to find today?" I ask.

Again, they both look at each other and Mrs. Lester mumbles something in Korean and Mr. Lester mumbles something in Spanish which I *did* understand, but I won't repeat in this book.

Finally, I just ask them if they would like to come into my office and have a seat to discuss what it is that they are looking for. I don't even know if they realize where they are and if they know that we build homes.

After a long and awkward silence, Mr. Lester says, "My wife doesn't speak any English. She can understand a little but can't speak. She's Korean. But she wants to know every word you say so I'm going to try to translate to her."

Great! A breakthrough! He can speak Korean, and we can all have a nice conversation and figure how to make this miserable couple happy. Surprisingly enough, Mr. Lester initiates the conversation by saying that they need a large single-story that can accommodate his wheelchair. Therefore, it needs to be ADA (American Disability Association) approved. He tells me a little more about what she wants and what he wants. So I have a pretty good idea about which house we can build for them.

I finish my first spiel about what we have that can work for them. Mr. Lester turns to Mrs. Lester (who has been staring at me like I was an alien and giving her husband dirty looks the whole time) and begins to talk to her very loudly and extremely slowly . . . in *English*!

"*She said . . . she has a big . . . house she can . . . sell us!! It has four . . . bedrooms . . . and two . . . and a half . . . bathrooms!*" he yelled at her.

I can't believe this! He doesn't speak Korean? How do they even have a marriage? Is this some kind of a joke? Oh gosh, this is going to be excruciating.

After Mr. Lester gave her his "explanation" she made a "psssshhhh" sound and waved in his face and started yelling at him in Korean. He looked at me embarrassed and then started yelling at her in Spanish. Again, I cannot repeat what he called her, but it was some of the worst cussing I've ever heard!

Then he turned back to me and said in the calmest voice, "That sounds fine. We'd like to know what kind of time frame that we'd be looking at."

So I tell him that since we'll be making some significant changes to the plan, it will take about eight to nine months to build.

Suddenly, Mrs. Lester came alive and stood up and yelled angrily at me saying something that sounded like "Ye voo?" over and over again. I just looked at Mr. Lester and I frantically said, "Can you tell her what I said?"

Again, he straightened himself up in his wheelchair and took a deep breath, looked at his wife and yelled slowly, accentuating every syllable, "*She said . . . she can finish . . . the house . . . in eight . . . to nine . . . months!*"

Weirdly enough, she must have understood this and definitely did not like it because she pushed him backward into the wall and said in perfect English with a brilliant Korean accent, "Oh, you crazy f_ _ _!" (Insert the worst *F* word imaginable.)

Oh my god! I was seriously trying not to cry or laugh or snort. This poor guy! What kind of life was this that he was leading? His wife is only practicing cuss words in English and can't speak or understand anything else except what she just yelled at the top of her lungs? At this point, I'm just hoping that they are upset at each other enough to just leave. And boy, did they!

She is repeatedly calling him a "crazy f_ _ _," while he is yelling at her and fighting her off as much as he can because she is climbing over him to get hold of the wheelchair handles so she can push him out. She finally climbs over him, gets behind the wheelchair, and starts to violently push him out of my office while he is desperately trying to hold on to his wheels and slow her down. The entire time, they are yelling at each other in different languages. She's almost tipped him over twice, and I stand up to help steady him. I'm honestly about to take this lady out. She's being so mean to him.

He looks at me while his wife is pushing him as hard as she can and calmly says, "We'll come back out to visit with you later," and then continues yelling in Spanish while she's pushing him way too fast and too hard out the front door. She races him down the ramp and is still screaming at him. I watched, even though it was painful, to make sure that she didn't hurt him when he was getting into the car. She was obviously still mad because she peeled out while looking at him and screaming and not even looking at the road.

Mr. and Mrs. Lester came back in a better mood, but it was such a painful process while we built their home. I've never witnessed such screaming, yelling, and cussing at each other. Every time they came in was like that, and they became the scary people on the block who would yell obscenities at the neighbor's kids for playing in their driveway. Thank goodness no one can understand them! I still think about them and hope that things are a little better and they haven't killed each other yet.

I'd Like to Waste
a Terrible Mime

Recently, I met a young man who was very excited about buying a new home. He was a very animated person and barely had time to talk about what he wanted in a new home because he couldn't stop talking about his church. He just wanted to spread the word to everyone, and according to him, God would provide him whatever he wanted because he had dedicated his life to religion. This is actually a very normal thing. I have people who come in all the time and tell me that God told them as they were driving by a certain house that it was theirs.

So I was really enjoying this conversation and we finally began to talk about the house. He said that he has five children whom he needed to support and he wanted them to each have their own room. He was a single guy, so he wanted a great master's bedroom if he was ever blessed enough to receive another wife. (It's refreshing to hear someone say that a wife would be a blessing.) (That last part was sarcasm.) We decided that we had a home that would fit his needs and have a great closet for his future blessed wife.

Now it was time to start talking about the almighty dollar. Every time we have this discussion, things tend to get interesting. I let him know that his monthly payment would be around $1,500, and he said, "I'm not worried about it. God will provide for me and my family."

So I asked him what he did for a living and did not realize that I was going to get a Broadway show for an explanation. He stood up, bent his knees, started looking around like he was crazy and then started moving his hands like he was trapped in a box.

He pushed the door open to his imaginary box and then I guess his box was hanging from an imaginary rope because he grabbed the rope and started pulling himself along the rope all over my office. The rope ended behind my chair where he pulled an imaginary flower out of his imaginary pocket, smelled it, and handed it to me.

I didn't want to cater to this stupidity so I just smiled at him with my best "fake smile and get the heck out of here" look. The smile wasn't what he wanted. He just kept smiling weirdly and bending over closer to hand me the flowers.

Oh god. I was going to have to accept these stupid flowers. So I slowly and embarrassingly took the flowers and said "Thank you," while looking down at my shoes because I suddenly felt like a complete idiot.

When I said, "Thank you," he bowed as if to royally say, "You're welcome." I just kept hoping that this ridiculous show was over. It wasn't. He grabbed his imaginary rope again and pulled himself back over to his chair, opened the door to his box, sat down in his box, looked around all sad, and then held his hands out in the air as if to say, "I'm back in the box. What do you think?"

Let me first just add that he was a terrible mime. So I said dryly, "You're a mime."

He said, "Yeah! How'd you guess?" He laughed a psychotic laugh that made me wish I was packing heat on a hip holster just in case he pulled out an imaginary knife.

As much as I wanted him to leave, I humored him and asked him where he was a mime around here. He said that he mimed at his church. He mimed the hymns while the congregation sang.

Now, I've been to church my whole life and never in all my thirty-five years did I ever say to myself, "I could totally understand these words to this music if someone was acting it out or miming it badly at the front of the church."

Looking back on this experience, I can't believe that I asked him the next question. "How do you mime a hymn?"

Instead of answering me, he did something that I hoped he wouldn't do. He stood up again and sang and acted out a hymn that I had never heard before. Let me just add that he is a far better mime than a singer.

Enough with this imaginary mess, let's find out if he makes a good living as a mime. I think I know the answer. I asked him what he made per month, and he said it's different every month, but some Sundays he makes more than $150. But he says that he will be provided with what he wants because of his godly lifestyle.

So I did a mime of my own and put my hands up in the air and said, "I can't help you." He was sad but vowed to save up all his offering money and come back and buy the house with cash. I said, "I'll see you then." I didn't feel bad because I knew he could build an imaginary house and be just as happy as if he was trapped in a real one.

LINDA MAGENTA

One of my very first customers after I started in new home sales was probably my most memorable and most referenced by my friends and colleagues. She is truly a legend in the sales community, and I loved her for who she was and I still see her and talk to her to this day. This is the simple story of a woman with a dream who made that dream come true. But the road to realization was paved with hilarity and so much explaining that I thought twice about continuing this job.

Linda Griffin walked into my model home one day, and she was the nicest person I may have ever met. She said, "Well, hello, beautiful young lady. I just want to go into the house next door. I drive by it every day, and I finally decided to stop by and take a look at the inside. This is my dream house! I know it's going to be beautiful. I'll never be able to buy something like this but I still like to dream, you know?"

I said, "Most people start out with a dream and then they make it a reality. Why do you think that you can't have that home?"

"I don't make enough money and I think that my credit is really bad. I like to buy furniture and write a check for it when I know I don't have enough money to cover it when it goes through," she said with a knowing sly grin.

I laughed and said, "Yeah right," and laughed again and then it turned into a nervous laugh because I could tell from the look on her face that she was serious. So now I know she's a serial hot check writer, and I just concluded with an awkward, "Oh, okay. That's one way to get furniture. You can go in and take a look around."

"Thanks," she said and headed out the door and to the walkway to the model home we called the Magenta.

Over an hour later, I was working away and realized that she never came back through the office to leave. At this model complex, it was all fenced in and you had to come back by the office to get in and out. I just thought that maybe she had hopped the fence and left a long time ago. I looked outside and her car was still there. *What the heck?* I thought to myself.

As much as I dreaded a weird "get out" conversation, I made my way over to the Magenta. When I walked in the door, Linda was sitting on an ottoman and had a dreamy and teary look on her face.

She jumped up and said, "Oh! I'm so sorry. I just can't leave. This is my house! This is my house! I want this house. I don't ever want to leave cuz this is my home!"

So I talked to her for a while and found out that she was a guard at a local women's prison and didn't make too much money, but her ex-husband was in the military. She was a single mom with three kids to take care of, and we talked about what she can do over the next year to be able to buy the Magenta. She said she was going to do it. I wanted to believe her, most of the time, people don't do what they're told in order to fix their credit.

Literally, for the next year, Linda came by at least four times a week and just sat in the model for twenty minutes to sometimes over two hours. Every time she would come in, I would just wave and say, "Hey Linda! See ya in an hour or so!"

She would laugh and would just go sit. The funny thing was she talked to other buyers who came in and out of the model, and they thought she was crazy but in a heart-warming way. She talked a lot of people into buying the Magenta home plan.

Over a year went by, Linda and I talked about how to get her credit fixed and during that time she was a constant fixture. One day she walked in with a young gentleman in tow. He was a realtor. Linda had gotten approved for a house and she was barely approved for the starting price of the Magenta! It was bare bones with no upgrades. I was about to get to know Brenda really well. She was finally going to get her Magenta.

Now, remember, the only house Linda has ever seen or been in contact with was the Magenta. So when she sat down in front of me, she said, "I want my Magenta now. I want that house. I've been waiting every day for a year, and I want it."

I said, "Well, we'll have to build you a Magenta plan. We don't have the one next door for sale yet. We'll have to build it from the ground up."

"What do you mean?" she said. "I want the Magenta. I did everything you told me to do over the last year and I want to buy that house. You told me I could have *that* house. The Magenta," she whimpered, holding back tears and pointing toward the model home.

Little did I know that was just the first of many things that she didn't understand. I said, "Brenda, everyone who decides they want the Magenta has to build it somewhere else. You even get to pick all your colors and even pick out a *lot* where you want it to be built on!"

"A lot? A lot of what? I don't want a lot of anything except a Magenta. What are you talking about . . . a lot?" She asked with a scrunched up face like I was speaking an alien language.

Confused that anyone could not know what a *lot* was, I said, "A *lot* is the piece of land that you build your house on."

"What? I don't understand." She looked at her realtor with a confused look on her face like I was making something up and she had to make sure that I was telling the truth. At this, her realtor basically said the same thing that I had just said, and she shook her head, obviously not understanding.

So I said, "Let's just jump in the car and try to find a lot . . . um . . . land that you like."

At this she said, "Okay, but I still don't know what you talkin' about. What do I need a lot of?"

I knew we were in for a long day if I had to explain legal terms of a contact to her later, and her understanding of a "lot" had not progressed in the least. Sigh.

Linda, her realtor, and I jumped in my car and began to drive through the neighborhood toward the infamous available *lots*. The next few statements that Brenda made had me baffled for a few seconds until I realized what she was actually thinking.

Looking around as if she was at a drive-through zoo and exotic animals were all around the car, she finally says, "All these Magentas look different. Look over there at that Magenta. It's a one-story Magenta. That Magenta is a two story that looks different than my Magenta! Look at that one! How do I know what my Magenta is going to look like? How do you even know what Magenta I want? See! Look at that Magenta! It looks totally different than the Magenta that I want. Oh god! What are ya'll doing to me?"

The car was completely silent except for the sound of the wheels in mine and the realtor's head trying to figure out what in the heck she was talking about. It took me seriously about thirty seconds to realize that she thought every house in the neighborhood was called a Magenta! Oh my gosh! How do I deal with this? How do I explain this when we haven't even been able to get past the concept of a lot?

I said, "Linda. We sell ten different houses, and each of those have different names. It just so happens that the house that you like is called the Magenta. The Magenta is a two-story plan. We have some one story plans, but they have different names."

After a long, awkward pause, she said, "I don't know what you talkin' bout, but all I want is that Magenta. I don't want any of those other houses that you talkin' bout. John (realtor), can you make sure that she builds me a Magenta? There's too many Magentas around here for ya'll to be playing around with all these other houses when you know all I want is *my* Magenta!" she said in a perplexed tone that I thought was humorous because this was the silliest conversation that I've had since I was born.

As if she didn't even hear the answer that I just gave or she just totally ignored it, she looked out the window again and said, "Ooh . . . that Magenta is really pretty, but I don't like the Magenta next to it. Can you build me a Magenta that looks like that one?"

Fortunately, the *Magenta* that she liked was actually a *Magenta* plan so I could truthfully tell her "Yes!"

We finally get to the area where we're currently building, and I told her to look out her window and look at the lots and see if anything pops out to her.

She says, "What am I looking at again? I just want a house. I don't know about the 'lotta' stuff you talking about. What am I supposed to do?"

Knowing that this could go on all day, I finally just say, "Why don't we build your house on this lot . . . er . . . uh . . . piece of land? It doesn't have a lot premium on it so we have more room for options and upgrades."

There was an uncomfortable silence and I realize that I had just said a sentence that completely blew her mind. She said, "I understood three words that you just said. Please help me and speak English."

So the realtor and I picked her lot, helped her pick her interior design colors and we explained the contract so that she understood it. It went like this: "If you want the Magenta just like the one next door, initial here twenty-seven times and sign here fourteen times." She understood that and gladly signed.

Weekly phone calls telling her the construction updates became the highlight of my week. My construction manager and I tried to explain to her what was happening, and we'd make bets as to how many "Whats," "Huhs," and "I don't get its" she would say.

I still see Linda Magenta every once in a while. She came out to the new model where I was working a couple of years ago and I thought, "Oh gosh, she's going to sit in this house for a year!" But when I asked her if she wanted a new home, she said, "Girl no! You know I love my Magenta! But how much is this Magenta here?"

Is This a "Toot" Story Home?

One of the big rules of new home sales is not to judge a book by its cover. I've had several people pull up in a junker car, dirty clothes, and tattered-looking children who had hundreds of thousands of dollars in the bank! Recently, I met a couple whom I did not prejudge them upon their entrance into the model home. They had a few things right off the bat those were not going well for them, though.

Number 1, the gentleman probably weighed about four hundred pounds and she was probably close to three hundred pounds. Number 2, they drove up in a Geo Metro. If any of you don't remember the nineties when Geo Metros were a hot car, these might be the smallest car ever made and two of the largest people I've ever seen squeezed and shimmied out of it.

I'm not a small woman, but I bought a car that could fit my . . . largeness. I chose a husband who was taller and larger than me so I'd look smaller. I try to hang out with larger friends so that in pictures, I don't look like the biggest one! So I know what it's like to be larger than the average person. If you're the size of two people . . . don't pick a Geo Metro as your car. It's just a general rule of thumb.

I usually open the door for my customers, but feeling that I'd be standing in the doorway for an awkwardly long time while they levered themselves out of their car, I opted to stand looking out the door from the inside trying not to look like I'm gawking.

Suddenly, the phone rang and it broke me out of my trance. I ran to get it so my assistant opened the door for them and began talking with them. After I hung up the phone, I sat silently in my office and listened to the conversation. Here are a few things I heard before I came out to visit with them:

"My wife works at the Burger Palace. I just picked her up because she doesn't have a car."

"She brings home the money, I just sit at home and wait for her to cook me dinner."

"I'm retired. I don't work. I make her work." And he laughed a hearty laugh and then . . . *"Ppppppppppbbbbbbbbbbbbbbbbrrrrrrrrrrrrrrtttttt."*

What's that last statement you ask? Well, that would be the longest, loudest, and most drawn-out fart that I've ever heard in public. At this point, I knew that my assistant was going to need to excuse herself for a short burst of hysterical laughter. So I decided to come out of my office to relieve her.

I walk into the danger zone, take over, and begin talking with them about what they're looking for and how much they want to spend. Of course, they haven't discussed the money part of it yet but they want our largest home with all the upgrades. Sure. We all do. At this point, my assistant has ducked into my office to gag, barf, or both.

We walked into the model home and during my short conversation with them, this large man began sweating profusely, passed hellacious gas too many times to count and didn't flinch once, skip a beat, or indicate in any way that we all could hear and smell the toots during our conversation. I was completely in awe and was trying to find a way not to breathe through my nose and still hold a civil conversation. Here's how that conversation went.

"Oh! This is beautiful! How much . . . *pbbt* . . . does one of these run?" he asked.

"About $170,000," I said slowly, looking from him to his wife for any sort of acknowledgement that he just ripped a 6 on a 10-point scale for flatulence.

"Honey, you could really make some awesome dinners . . . *blllaaaarrrrrttttt* . . . in this kitchen!" he said. She just nodded.

"Oh, you are the cook (I'm interrupted by a tommy gun sound that obviously fired mud bullets) . . . in the family?" I said trailing off at the end. Surely, they realized that I at least heard *that* one when it interrupted me!

"Oh yes," she said. "I have to keep him happy." She laughed. He laughed too and at the same time a powerful burst blew out of his pants.

I laughed heartily, but I was really laughing about the fact that I was envisioning telling my coworkers about this when I got back to the office.

"I make her do all the work because I'm retired. I'm not going to do anything except . . . *ffffffffffffffttttttt* . . . lay around the house and watch my TV shows. That's the life!" he chuckled and she snorted in response to that one too.

"Well, I'm (I'm interrupted by a loud gurgly moan from his stomach) thinking maybe we need to see our other single story just to make sure (second gurgly lurch) that this house is the one," I said at this point, stifling a gag and praying to get outside.

The crazy part of it was how nonchalant he was about the whole thing. He was leaning against the breakfast bar in the model home just letting them rip and his wife didn't change expressions or let on to the fact that a disgusting green cloud was forming above our heads.

I was starting to get sick and was a few seconds away from bolting out of the room when I suddenly said, "Why don't we take a look at that other home that could work for you?" I started to walk toward the front door.

Once I turned my back to them, I actually gagged and was just hoping that nothing came out. He stopped me in the hallway and said, "I really like this home. I think this could work for us but we need some more . . . *pppbbbbbbbbbrrrrrtttt* . . . space to move around. Can I use your restroom?"

Ugggghhh! I wanted to scream. Is this a normal way of life for him that it's okay to just go around different places of business and pass horrific gas? And not even acknowledge that you're farting? As much as I wanted to know the answers to those questions, I used that as my cue to get the heck out of there. So I said, "Sure. Take your time," and walked out the door to go outside on the path back to my office.

My knees nearly buckled when I walked outside with gratefulness to the higher power for getting me out of that house. I know I had the most horrific look on my face because when I got back to the office, my assistant and a realtor friend of mine were in my office, and they both looked at me and asked what was wrong.

I told them what had just happened and was able to tell the long version because he was in the bathroom for twenty minutes. I purposefully stayed in my office that night until two hours after closing time because I wanted to give that deathly green fog in the bathroom every chance to dissipate before I braved the threshold of the model again.

When they finally came back into my office, obviously refreshed and six pounds lighter, they were ready to go see the house. For once in my life, I lied to a customer. I told them that I had customers who had just arrived and I would just give them the key to go look at it. I felt so bad but my stomach couldn't stand another minute of the flatulent buyer.

When they arrived back at the office, I asked them to go ahead and get their prequalification done so we could get started on the home they loved and the model. At this, the wife said that mortgage companies always tell them they can't have what they want. So I said, "Yeah. That's what they do, sometimes. Well, when you feel like you're ready, let me know."

She said she had to go home and cook her husband dinner because he was starving. I was so thankful they left. I'm sorry already! I have a very weak stomach and I gagged three times thinking about the whole thing while I was writing this story! No joke.

PARANORMAL APPRAISER

It was a gloomy, rainy day in Killeen, Texas, with a local builder; and I had already fielded two home loan appraisers who needed information when a third appraiser came to my office doorway during a meeting I was having with my construction superintendents. He was one of my favorite appraisers because he was a rancher and extremely friendly, and we always liked to see him appraise homes because he liked us too. We could always count on his appraisals to be right on cue. This day, he felt like sticking around and talking with me and my coworkers. His name was Bob Campbell.

I think today is the day that Bob Campbell lost it a little. I had remembered that the last time Bob came in was over a month ago, and he had said that he had been struck by lightning while he was baling hay on his ranch in the country, so he wasn't walking very well. That day I had been very busy, and I asked in passing if he was okay, and he said he was okay but he was still really sore. I remembered thinking how strange that was and how awful that would be because I've been about fifteen feet from being struck by a bolt of lightning, and I couldn't hear for a week, had headaches, and generally felt awful for a long time afterward.

I know that he obviously wanted to chitchat for a while by his leaning against the doorframe of my office door.

I obliged him much to the disdain of my coworkers. Although now they're glad that I started talking to him because they got to experience one of the weirdest conversations I've ever had with anyone in my entire life. So it all began like this:

"Well, how are you doing today, Bob?" I asked cheerfully.

"Well . . . I'm a little leery about being out in this rain today," he said.

"Oh, that's right! You said you had gotten struck by lightning last time you were in! I bet you're not feeling too well about that. How are you feeling?" I asked.

"I'm a little nervous about my ankle getting struck by lightning again. I think that I was transmitting from it the day that I got struck. Or they were transmitting to me," he said and started looking down at his ankle and moving it around like he was stretching it out.

What? I just stared at him, looked at the construction guys in front of me (who can't be seen by Bob from his angle) who were wide-eyed with shock. I was looking from Bob to them and then finally after enough awkward silence, I decided to make one of my famous comments to break the silence. I truly thought he was pulling our chain. Transmitting? What in the world is he talking about?

"Ummm . . . Bob. Do . . . you . . . mean . . . 'transmitting' as in the 'aliens' were talking to you?" I said in a totally funny and condescending way. The guys cracked up a little and I chuckled a little bit waiting for the punch line of this joke.

"No, not the aliens. The military," he said, without skipping a beat.

I just sat there and again looked back at the construction guys, one of them was staring ahead with his mouth gaping open and the other was chewing on a Styrofoam cup and trying not to laugh out loud. There were tears coming out of his eyes and dropping down his cheeks. So I decided I couldn't look at the guys anymore because my face suddenly hurt from needing to laugh. I took the bait.

"Bob, what do you mean the military was transmitting to you?" I asked slowly and quizzically because I still thought this could be a joke. Then the madness began. He began to tell a story that could be the plot line for the next *X-Files* movie.

"Back in '68, the military put a transmitter in my ankle. They realized that I had the ability to see into the future," he stated matter-of-factly.

At this moment, one of the construction guys left to go laugh in the hallway and the other one was still chomping down on his cup and rocking back and forth, red-faced, crying and trying not to make a sound.

He continued, "See, I'm part Cherokee Indian, so I naturally have the propensity to anticipate things. You should have seen me when I was playing football in high school! I could anticipate what the defense and the quarterback would do and be able to stop any play they did. My coach would always say, 'How did you know they were gonna do that?' And I always just said I didn't know. I just felt it.

"So I wanted to know just how good I could see into the future and predict things, so I took this test that twelve thousand other Cherokee Indians took, and I scored the second highest score out of all of them. That's how well I can anticipate the future."

I couldn't help it. I had to ask the next question, "Bob . . . um . . . are they transmitting to you now?"

Slowly and mystically, he said, "I . . . don't . . . know."

Not being able to hold things in any longer, Darrell, the construction guy who had been chomping on a cup, decided to test his anticipation skills and yelled, "BOO!" Then he looked at Bob and said, "Did you anticipate that?" and he absolutely fell off his chair laughing.

It was ridiculous, maniacal laughter because this was his chance to let everything out that he had been holding in, and it was my chance too. So I started dying laughing and crying. I had tears streaming down my face. Bob smiled but he was a man on a mission. He continued his story, even though Darrell was now looking at me and putting his foot up close to his mouth and pretending he was talking on the phone using his ankle. I can't tell you how hard it was not to laugh.

He continued. "So now, the government knows how well I could anticipate things and predict the future. The thing is that the transmitter in my ankle reads my subconscious thoughts. So I don't even know when I'm helping people. My subconscious knows when anyone around the world is in trouble and the government is able to hear my subconscious thoughts through the transmitter, and they can make a call and save the people who would have been about to die. Only bad thing is, they put this thing in my leg six months shy of being able to predict my brother being killed."

Okay. Here it was: Proof that Bob was having a bad flashback episode or some sort of a post-traumatic stress. I started to feel really bad for him at this point, and I asked if his wife knew about all of this and how she felt about the government being able to track him everywhere he went. I basically wanted to see if there was someone I could call who could come and help him if he flipped out here.

"Oh no! My wife doesn't even know about the transmitter!" he stated emphatically.

"What?" Darrell asked. "You mean, we're the only people who know about this? Is the government listening and going to kill us for knowing?" he asked, still trying to get him to talk more about it because he was having fun and at this time, recording the conversation with his phone because he knew no one would believe it.

I started trying to ask Bob questions that might bring him out of this state, but he kept on going and he truly believed this stuff. Part of me believes that something like this is possible yet so out-of-this-world unbelievable. So I asked him, "Bob, if they're still using your thoughts to help people, it doesn't seem fair. How are they going to pay you?"

"That's a good question and when I was lying in bed recuperating from being struck by lightning, I asked the 'powers that be' if my ankle was still transmitting after the lightning strike, and they told me it was. So then I asked them how I would get paid for all of the lives that I've saved since 1968, and they said that when I reached the age of sixty-five, I'm sixty-two now, that they will count up all the lives I've helped save all over the world by being able to read my subconscious thoughts, and they'll pay me that way."

Darrell and I just stared at each other, and finally he had to leave. He couldn't hold it in any longer, and I heard him explode in laughter out the back door. I was in shock and trying to figure out if Bob was okay to go back out into the real world. I didn't even know what to say to him anymore. He stated everything so matter-of-factly and he truly believed all of that craziness.

I was in a daze. Is this conversation really happening? I was trying to make sense of it all and say something to him that was rooted in the real world. So I said, "You better get on home and be safe and out of this weather. We don't want you to get struck by lightning again."

He said, "It would be the third time if I did. I was already struck by lightning once when I was about three years old. I was playing under front porch and lightning struck the house, knocked me out, and mama found me later and woke me up. No, sir. I don't want to get struck by that again. Of course, one of these strikes may stop it from transmitting. I don't want to get struck again though. Thirty days in the hospital is a long time, and they had to take my blood every twenty minutes to make sure I had enough medicine in me."

Not wanting to go any further with this, I told him that I needed to get to an appointment with a customer at their house and that he needed to go home and rest. He agreed and walked out the door and said, "Maybe I'm helping somebody right now. Never know. Have a good day!" And he left.

I just stood there, limp. Darrell came back in and sat down, and we stared at each other with gaping mouths for a good minute until my sales partner came in from being with a customer and he sat down and looked at both of us. I couldn't talk and the only thing Darrell could say was, "Dude! Dude! Dude!" He managed to scream them out between bouts of riotous laughter.

We finally were able to talk and told my sales partner that he had just missed the weirdest conversation ever and there were still about four more hours in the work day to go. I couldn't do anything but stare into space. I was so in shock and kept thinking about everything he said. I wrote every detail down with Darrell helping me recall things. I had my sales partner take all the customers while I got over the shock of it all.

As I write this, that was only two days ago. I hope that I'll be able to write a follow-up chapter and let you all know what happens when I see Bob again. The weird thing is Bob probably already knows that I'm writing a chapter about him. Hopefully, I don't have to pay him imaginary royalty money when he retires for all the people who have laughed at this story!

THE SALES ARE "OUTTA THIS WORLD!"

W hen you are in sales, you sometimes get lucky and get to work with a really great partner whom you become friends with and whom you can trust. I have been blessed throughout my career in that I am still good friends with all of my ex-sales partners. Oh . . . we've had our moments, but we always made up and never let business get in the way of friendship.

One of my past partners was such a character that I just had to write a chapter about him. I still bring many of my clients to him to this day and I know that they will have a great time. If they don't remember anything that day, they will remember Stevie. Stevie has never met a stranger and he treats you like a long-lost family member right when you walk in.

Before I get to the really weird stuff, I have to talk about some of the crazy sales techniques that Stevie uses. The last time I was in his office, I noticed that there was a minnow hanging from a thumbtack that was pushed into a nice framed painting sitting behind his desk. I asked, "Is that a small dead fish?"

He said, "Yeah! It keeps me motivated."

"To put a stick-up air freshener in your office?" I said smugly.

"Ha! Ha!" he said, obviously not amused. "I read a book about these fish market guys who make a great experience for their customers by being funny, different, and putting on a show. I want to be like that every day and make a great experience for everyone."

"By putting a dead fish on a picture behind you? Couldn't you find a more inconspicuous place to put it?" I asked, kind of grossed out.

"What do you mean?" he said. He honestly didn't think that was weird or gross.

So I left it alone and said, "Cool."

I always loved when it was Stevie's turn to greet a customer. He had a one-liner for everyone. During football season, no matter who walked in the door, he'd swing it open, get in a Broadway-style stance with his knees bent, arms opened out wide like he was waiting for a hug, and he'd yell, "How 'bout those Cowboys?"

Some people laughed. Some people yelled back, "How 'bout those Cowboys?" But most people were scared to death. One couple, I remember, he had to beg them to come back in and apologized for scaring them. I couldn't stop laughing while I was ducked under the desk in my office. I loved working with Stevie.

His other famous one liner was and still is, "Welcome to our neighborhood where all the women are good lookin' and all the kids are above average." Then he laughs and laughs like it's the first time he's ever said it and quite possibly the funniest words he's ever spoken.

The funny thing is, there's absolutely nothing to say to that except "What?" But it does give him a good icebreaker. People can't say they're "just looking" if they can't pick their jaw up off the floor.

Stevie is an avid guitar player and he's very talented at song writing as well. His last song was titled "Why You Wanna Treat Me Like a Dog Treats a Tree?" He often brings his guitar into the office and sings and plays his latest songs for his customers who just eat it all up! He really does have ingenious lyrics and a talent for the guitar.

The strangest thing that Stevie has ever said happened over a sushi lunch with the rest of the new home builder sales team sitting at the same table. Somehow, we all got to talking about ghosts and paranormal events. So during all these creepy stories, Stevie was really quiet and pensive. Then, he shocked the pants off everyone when he said this:

"Hey!" Stevie said without even looking up from his plate. "I've got a story that will beat all of those."

I'm thinking he's going to tell us some crazy ghost story, and we're all going to flip out. So I'm getting really excited and the whole table goes quiet because you can tell he's serious, and this is probably going to be good.

"This is the scariest thing that has ever happened to me and to this day, I don't know what the heck happened. I don't like to think about it and I've never even told anyone about it until now," Stevie said solemnly as his expression looked like he had gone someplace far away in his mind.

I got the chills. Oh man! This is gonna be good! Stevie is going to freak us all out with this scary story. Yes!

Stevie continues, "One night, my wife and I had a romantic evening on the beach. We had built a fire and were just talking and listening to the waves crash. We had drunk a few bottles of wine . . ."

Hold up! Just the two of them . . . drank *a few* bottles of wine? I thought to myself, *Well, whatever happens, the explanation is . . . alcohol.*

"We had drunk a few bottles of wine, and the next thing I knew . . ." Stevie started to choke up like it was hard to even think about it.

Wow! This must have really scared him.

At this point, you could hear a pin drop and we were all waiting to hear about the ghost that he saw or some crazy paranormal event.

Stevie regained his composure and said, " . . . the next thing I knew, I was waking up with my pants around my ankles, my wife's pants were around her ankles and I felt violated." Stevie then looked down dramatically and said something that we all were stunned by. "I think we were abducted by aliens and probed."

It was so quiet and I, for one, was waiting for the punch line. I kept waiting. There wasn't one. He was serious but I couldn't believe it. Not yet. So in classic Myka style, I said, "Stevie . . . you passed out and were molested by a beach hobo."

The whole table erupted in laughter except for Stevie. His mind was still there in that moment and he truly was traumatized by that event. But now, he had to laugh because the whole place was screaming and hooting with laughter.

Stevie kept yelling at everyone, "It's true! It's true! I swear to God!"

Finally, I said, "Stevie, if you can't remember, how do you *know* it's true?"

"Because they still visit us! At our house! We'll wake up in the middle of the night and hear a weird sound and then we'll see a window open that wasn't open before," he said in a pleading voice.

I thought that I'd have to play along so I just said, "Well, that sucks for you. I hope they don't probe you again."

What the heck do you say to that? You wake up at the beach after *a few* bottles of wine, your pants down, feeling violated, no memory of what happened and you automatically think its aliens? That's not what I would think of immediately. I'm taking my butt to the hospital to do a CSI probe to help my case against a wandering beach hobo predator posing as an alien. But that's just me.

Every time I see Stevie now, I ask him if he's been violated by aliens lately. He just cracks up and says no, but then I see the faraway look in his eye and the way he shifts his weight in his chair, and I wonder, "Is he really being visited?"

My question was answered in the epilogue to this story. Read on.

EPILOGUE
TO STEVIE'S STORY:
THE SALES ARE
"OUTTA THIS WORLD!"

I just recently had lunch with Stevie after I had written his chapter, and I had to write the epilogue. I laughed until I cried that day, and I knew I had to share his latest story in this book. So that day at lunch, Stevie's epilogue went like this:

"I got a little drunk the other night with some of my neighbors down the street. For whatever reason, I decided to walk back down to my house, and by the time I got home, it was such a nice night that I decided to lay down on my lawn chair outside. It seemed like a perfect night to take all my clothes off except my underwear and enjoy a night under the stars," he said.

"Oh no!" I said laughing. "Don't you learn?"

"Yeah right!" he said. "I guess not! But anyway, so I'm lying there with my clothes off and just my tighty whities on, and I guess I go to sleep."

"You mean you passed out?" I said sarcastically.

"Whatever. I was tired and it was a gorgeous night," Stevie said. "After a while, I woke back up when my wife came home and I saw the headlights from her car. I kind of forgot that I didn't have any clothes on, and I met her in the driveway walking sleepily while she stared at me and turned off the car."

"She yelled from the car, 'What the heck are you doing naked on the driveway?' When she asked me that, I looked down, saw that I was only in my underwear, and my immediate thought was, *Holy crap! It happened again! I was abducted by aliens!*"

He continued, "My wife yelled at me to get in the car. She kept asking, 'Where are your clothes?' I seriously couldn't remember. So we backtracked the way I had walked home from the party. No clothes in the street. We even went back to our friends' house to see if I had stripped there before walking home. No clothes. So we went back home, and we both went to bed very uneasy about how I had gotten naked and was just wandering around the driveway in the middle of the night."

"The next morning, I went out to have my coffee on the back patio, and I saw my clothes had been perfectly folded on the lawn chair. I don't remember doing that, but I guess anything can happen."

After he finished his story, I sat there for a while thinking about this story and the story from the beach, and I told him to lay off the alcohol. Then I got serious and said, "Well, this time did you feel violated?"

He said, "No. But that doesn't mean it didn't still happen."

FLUFFY BUNNY SLIPPERS

I had been assigned a new sales partner a few years ago (while working for a local builder) who had come from working at a really high-end country club. She had been selling golf memberships to extremely rich people and schmoozed them with wine, cheese, and free golf pro sessions.

They loved her! She was a great sales person. But she decided to go from golf sales and country club memberships to new home sales in Killeen, Texas, where the average home sales price at that time was around $100,000. This was no country club with half million to million-dollar homes and homeowners. These are real people. She was in for a drastic change.

First off, if you are not familiar with soap operas, you need to Google the character Nicky Newman from *The Young and the Restless*; and he is exactly what my ex-partner and friend, Callie, looks like. She even had a fake blonde ponytail that went all the way down her back. If they were to make a reality show about *The Real Killeen Housewives*, she would be the star character! Callie had no idea what to expect when she made the big change!

One of the first days she was on the job, a young couple came in and the wife was in a see through white T-shirt with no bra, her husband's boxers, uncombed hair, and pink fluffy bunny slippers. I was sitting in my office with a perfect view of the show and enjoying every minute of it.

Callie stumbled all over her words because everyone wore a bra at the country club, pants over their boxers, had thousand-dollar combed extensions in their hair, and never wore their bunny slippers unless Gucci or Dior made them. They don't.

I remember her icebreaker of a greeting went something like this:

She looked at the husband who was dressed perfectly fine, not up to country club standards by any means though, and said, "Did you drag your poor wife out of bed to come look at houses?"

He looked confused and dryly said, "No."

His unkempt wife said nothing but glared at the sales rep/soap opera queen. I think at that point, Callie told the wife that she liked her bunny slippers and wished she could wear those to work. That seemed to ease the tension a little bit. After the painfully awkward greeting, Callie decided to take them to see an available home. Before she left, she looked at me like, "You better come with me! Don't leave me alone with these people!"

I just shrugged my shoulders and let her experience this on her own. This was a good initiation for Callie. She glared at my shrug and slammed the door when she walked out.

She came back shortly and without the customers in tow, marched into my office, stood in front of me, and put her hands on her hips with an, "I ought to kick your butt!" look on her face.

"What happened?" I asked with a sly grin.

"Well . . . ," she started. "We no more than got into the house when the wife bends over, grabs her stomach, and starts to moan, 'I feel sick!' I asked her if she was okay and she said she was pregnant. So I congratulated her and told her I was sorry she was sick. Without saying a word, she just fell down on the floor and started moaning and writhing around holding her stomach. I couldn't believe it! Then . . . the husband looked at me without even checking to make sure his wife was okay and says, 'Okay. Let's go look upstairs. She'll be fine.'

"Oh my god! What is wrong with these people? His wife is about to give birth on our upgraded carpet and he wants to look upstairs?"

"I told him, no, we need to stay with her and maybe call an ambulance and he said, 'She does that all the time. She's fine. She's not due for another six months. Ain't nothing gonna happen right now.'"

"Oh my god, Myka! What the heck is wrong with these people? We were walking around upstairs talking about the house and we couldn't even hear ourselves speak from the moaning downstairs! To top it all off, when he came downstairs, he says to his wife, 'I love this house, baby.' She actually moaned 'Me too, baby' while she was on the floor on her side holding her stomach."

"Then he said, 'You ready?' and she got up and got in the car and they drove off and said they'd think about it."

"What just happened? Is this normal? I don't think I can do this," she said, deflated.

I was thoroughly enjoying this story and told her to get used to this kind of thing, that this is the real world. The country club is a bubble in fantasy land. Weird stuff happens here in the real world all the time.

Callie got over her fear of the new world, and she's become a fiercely successful custom home sales representative. Just to give her crap, almost every time I see her, I walk in and grab my stomach and start moaning. She calls me a few choice words and then gives me a hug. She hasn't seen any more fluffy bunny slippers, but she still has to deal with boxers hanging out of baggy pants and braless women. She's learned to deal with it though and calls me every time she has a non-country club experience or if someone nearly gives birth on her upgraded custom model home floor.

Sales, Lies, and Videotapes

In a previous chapter, I told you about the sales manager who told me to get on a treadmill as my goal for the week. He said he was tired of watching the entire sales force get fat. He also looked at my swollen turned ankle, looked at the other ankle, and said he couldn't tell the difference.

Actually, he's a very nice person, and he was a great manager. He had a few hilarious quirks though. We will call him Derek. Derek is probably the most paranoid person I've met in my whole life. The reason he takes any precaution is so it won't have a dire and catastrophic end that he has gloriously imagined could happen.

For instance, when I got hired, he told me a lot of things. One of them was that I should keep every piece of paper I write on and every contract that I write. "This builder has an underground bunker where they've kept everything they've done for fifty years in case they get sued," he said. I thought that was kind of weird. An underground bunker? Really?

He also told me that there are hidden cameras everywhere in the model homes and outside the model homes. If I'm late to work, he'll know it. If I pick my nose at my desk, he'll know it. If I don't close a deal and let a good customer walk out, he'll know it!

I remember thinking, *Oh my god! This is crazy! I better stay on my toes.*

Now I just laugh and think how gullible I was.

For the first few weeks, I was early to work every day. I was a model sales representative. I remember the first day that I was late to work. I had wrecked my husband's truck. I ran into the dumpster and punched a hole into the back of it and spent several minutes trying to get it unstuck from the dumpster and spent even more minutes crying uncontrollably.

I was about ten minutes late when I pulled up to the model home. Just as I was putting the key in the door, my phone rang. It's Derek. I answer and try to sound like I'm not rattled.

Derek says, "Good morning. What are you doing?" in a singsong, sarcastic kind of irritating voice.

I said, "I'm sitting at my desk logging into the computer." A lie.

"No, you're not," he says, matter-of-factly.

"I'm not?" I said with a defeated tone.

"No. You're just getting to the model. Late. And you're opening the front door. Late," he said, irritatingly accurate.

I start to look around to see where he's parked. How does he know that? There's no one around!

"Where are you?" I asked.

I'm starting to get a little weirded out thinking he's stalking me and is going to jump out of a bush or something any second with a cloth soaked in chloroform.

"I'm everywhere," he said. "Just remember that."

Click. Dial tone.

That same scenario happened a couple more times over the next few months. After a couple of months, a new sales girl showed up. It was Callie; who has a disdain for fluffy bunny slippers. He obviously told Callie the same load of bologna because she walked into the model home looking in every nook and cranny for a camera. She cried the first day because she didn't want anyone to watch her while she was working. She though it was weird.

I told her that I didn't think it was true that it was just a scare tactic. She said that Derek told her he was about to install fingerprint recognition on our computers so we had to put our fingers in every morning and no one else could log in for us. I'm sure retina scans were next on the list.

The only way to get Derek off your back and stop stalking you was to tell him that you were feeling sick. He was so paranoid about germs that he'd try to get on the other side of the town from you to avoid getting sick. He would shake your hand and immediately rub it down with hand sanitizer. That was one of those things that made you feel like a dirty low-life scum.

Despite all the quirks, he was a great manager and I have a lot of great memories with him in them. I recently spoke with him over the phone and told him I would be writing a chapter about him in my book. He laughed and said he couldn't wait to read it.

As we began to rehash some of the things he used to tell us about the video cameras and the underground bunkers, we laughed and just as we were about to hang up the phone he said, "Yeah. You wouldn't believe some of the videos that I have of you. I know all the crazy stuff you did and all the terrible Elvis songs you sang. Got 'em . . . all right here."

I tried to laugh and shrug it off, but he still makes me paranoid. God, I hope there are no videos.

THE DEADLY
DUNG BEETLE

This is a story about the second day in my life that I nearly died. I can't remember when I've been more scared! I can't believe that I made it to the office safely without killing myself and everyone around me. Here is how I nearly died that day.

It was a typical day for real estate; I was meeting a home inspector at a home in downtown Killeen. It is a beautiful property with gorgeous trees that are so old and tall. Nearly the entire yard is shaded. It's lovely.

So when I was standing in the driveway under a massive oak tree talking with the inspector about what he felt were the main issues with the house, the inspector said the main thing was that there was a massive hornets' nest in the breaker box and they got very angry with him when he opened it. He was not stung, but he did bother them a bit.

I am extremely allergic to hornets, wasps, and bees and mainly just hate them in general. I got the chills when he told me, and I could just imagine them stalking me at that very moment! We were still discussing the hornets when something big thudded on my right shoulder and I screamed and nearly jumped into the inspectors arms. (That would've been really bad since he was half my size.)

I looked on my shoulder. Nothing. I looked all around me where whatever it was could've fallen onto the ground after hitting my shoulder. Nothing. I thought it must've been a big acorn that fell from the tree and I didn't see where it went. The inspector said, "I hope it's not a hornet!" and laughed. We shook hands, said our goodbyes, and I walked back down the driveway across the street and into my car.

I had about a ten-minute drive down the main drag in Killeen until I was back at the office. Suddenly, the top of my head started to itch. So I scratched it. I didn't think anything of it. Then . . . the top of my head started to *really* itch, and I could tell that something *big* was in my hair on the top of my head.

Just like in a horror movie, everything turned into slow motion! I slowly looked at the top of my head in the rearview mirror and saw a giant orange-and-black bug moving around in my hair!

Orange and black! Orange and black! Oh my god! It's a hornet! A hornet! A hornet is in my hair, in my car! I started to scream at the top of my lungs and weirdly just screamed the word, "Hornet!" over and over again. I was in shock. Then it started to get mad and buzzed loudly trying to get loose from my hair!

Here are the thoughts that went through my head:

1. I can't touch it! It'll get mad and sting me!
2. It'll get mad and sting my head over and over again because it's stuck!
3. It'll get loose and fly around all pissed off and sting me while I'm driving and I'll wreck.
4. If I leave it alone, it'll make its way down to my face and sting my face!
5. Then it'll get pissed and fly around the car, sting me again and cause me to wreck the car.

I was panicking! So . . . the only rational thing I could think of was to roll the window down, stick my head out of the car as far as I could, and scream, "Get out! Get out! Get out!" while crying uncontrollably and driving down the main street in Killeen!

At this point, people in the cars around me were staring and wondering what in the world was going on. I was screaming with my head out the window and praying out loud for God to get this hornet out of my hair.

I pulled my head back into the car after a couple of minutes and in typical movie slow motion again, looked into the rearview mirror to see if it had flown out. There it was. And now . . . it was tangled even worse in my hair and was even more angry than before and was buzzing like crazy trying to break free from my hair!

I started to scream and cry uncontrollably. I didn't stick my head out of the car this time but people were still looking at me because my window was down and they could hear me screaming and asking God to get this hornet out of my hair! I was still screaming and crying, "Get out! Get out!"

As I approached my office, I slowly picked up the phone and called my partner, CJ. He answered calmly of course, and then I screamed, "CJ! There's a hornet in my hair! Oh my god, there's a hornet in my hair! Meet me in the parking lot *now* and get it out!"

CJ said calmly, "Do what?"

"There's a hornet in my hair! There's a hornet in my hair! Just get out in the parking lot now and get it out! Now! Now! Now!" And I hung up the phone, careened into the parking lot, threw the car into park, jumped out of the car, and bent over in front of CJ who was already in the parking lot ready to help.

I was screaming at him, "Get it out! Get it out! Get it out!"

He kept saying he didn't see it. Then it buzzed and he said, "Here it is." Next, he flipped out a giant bug that landed on the parking lot. It was an enormous dung beetle.

CJ pointed at it, looked at me and then said, "Well, there you go." He turned around and slowly walked back into the office, leaving me on my knees in the parking lot still in shock, heaving and weak from the adrenaline that had been pumping through my body. I looked at that dung beetle and was so glad it wasn't a hornet, but the dung beetle is just as scary and gross.

Everyone in the neighboring offices and businesses were staring and wondering what in the heck was going on with the screaming idiot who just pulled a giant beetle out of her hair and is now heavily breathing and crying on her knees in the parking lot . . . alone.

I took a picture of the dung beetle to remember the bug that nearly killed me. I can't believe I was able to drive that long, in panic mode, screaming with my head sticking out the window! My head keeps itching now, and everyone keeps saying that it probably laid eggs in my hair. If so, I'll write a follow-up chapter when the eggs hatch and I try to drive back to the office and have CJ kill the hatchlings. Hands down, scariest ten-minute drive ever. I hate bugs.

Here it is. The dung beetle that nearly killed me. I hope he died a horrible death being dismembered slowly by a ravenous bird. Uggh.

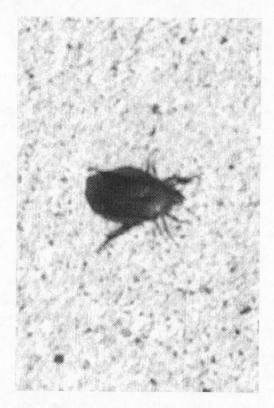

BAT GUANO CRAZY

I use the word *guano* in place of another far worse word that my clients chose to name the seller of the home that they were buying. As you have read by now, crazy people are littered throughout this book. Well, these sweet little first-time home buyers had never experienced it until it knocked on their door and tried to bust its way into their home!

We had negotiated a contract and were just waiting to close on it and get the keys so that my first-time home buyers could move into their home. They were so excited! Then . . . the seller went crazy. She decided halfway through the process that she needed more money but we had all agreed on the price and there was no going back. Her realtor gave up trying to work with her. I even met her with the permission of her realtor to help counsel her through it.

We met one night at Starbucks, and there was no calming her. She yelled at me and told me she was divorced, a single mom, and needed every dime she could get her hands on. I described to her that the thing about a contract is that it is legally binding and there is nothing that can be done or changed. I felt so bad about the situation that the listing realtor and myself gave up some of our commission so she would make a little bit more money at closing. That wasn't enough for her.

One windy cool night, she decided to defer going through her realtor or through me, the buyers' realtor and headed straight to the source. She found out my clients' address, went over to their house at nine o'clock at night, and began yelling at my sweet buyers to stop being greedy and give her more money! I know. The irony is classic.

The wife (of my home buyers) called me and said that I wouldn't believe what was going on out on the front porch of her home. She held the phone up for me to listen to the frantic ranting of a mad woman, the seller. I told her to hang up the phone and call the police. She did.

The wife then yelled down and told the crazy seller that she had called the police and told her to leave; they had kids who were sleeping.

Bat "Guano" Barton (Barton was the seller's last name) remained steadfast and was now screaming and taunting the wife to come downstairs like a real woman and fight her instead of chickening out and calling the cops!

At this point, the husband had had enough and told her it would be a good idea for her to leave before the cops got there; then he slammed the door on her.

She stayed there for a while screaming in rage on their front porch, then she got in her car and left. My little home buyers told the cops what happened but did not press any charges.

Bat "Guano" Barton was a tyrant for the rest of the process, knowing she was trapped in a contract and no one felt sorry enough for her to give her more money even when both realtors in the deal gave half of their money back to her.

My first-time home owners are happy in their new home, the other realtor and I laugh about this deal gone horribly wrong all the time but are so glad that it's over.

I saw Bat "Guano" Barton in passing the other day and said, "Hello!" in the friendliest and brightest way I knew how. It took her a second, but then she recognized me and gave me a horrible, go to hades look. I laughed but still feel awful for her. There are some people who are crazy and then there's *bat "guano" crazy*. Once you've gone *bat "guano" crazy*, there's no going back!

PART II

Elvis Presley
The King Lived in Killeen, Texas
So . . . I Bought His House

ALL SHOOK UP
AT THE KING'S HOUSE

When I was growing up, the only music I was allowed to listen to were Disney records, Tennessee Ernie Ford, Hank Williams Senior, the Statler Brothers, and Elvis Presley Gospel. My father is a Baptist preacher and was pretty strict about what we listened to. I remember, I saved up all my money one year and went to the mall and bought Michael Jackson's *Thriller* on cassette tape. It was awesome! One afternoon, my dad snapped it in half and stomped on it like it was a vile and filthy stinging bug, and said, "He's not going to sing a song in my house!"

Needless to say, I learned how to sing from the classic greats! If you ask anyone who knows me in this town who my favorite singer of all time is, they'll tell you without hesitation, Elvis Presley! When I was finishing up with college, I started singing in bands and sang professionally for about six years. Every band I was in, we did some sort of tribute to Elvis at the end of the night. No one else ever put as much heart and soul into music as he did. I still get the chills when I hear his songs.

Elvis Presley used to live in Killeen, Texas. Yes. You heard that right. How come you didn't know this? It's sad, I know. Everyone should know this! We should still have signs everywhere in Killeen! There used to be a sign up in Killeen a long time ago before you came into town that said, "Elvis lived here. So can you."

I love that! Where did it go? I can't say. But . . . when a local realtor came into my office where I was selling homes at the lake and told me that the house Elvis used to live in was available for sale . . . I nearly hit the ceiling!

It took me all of thirty seconds to find out where it was and run over there to look at it. It was a beautiful single story home on a half-acre with gorgeous trees that shaded the whole lot. The house sat back from the street with a big covered front porch. I could just imagine Elvis's pink Cadillac sitting in the driveway and people standing in the street just to catch a glimpse of him.

The house was in really good shape and a lot of the same fixtures were there. It was rumored that he had put in pink toilets. Those were not there, of course. I had remembered a photo of Elvis taken in front of the fireplace of the house he stayed in while he was in basic training on Fort Hood. This is it! I was standing in the exact same place Elvis stood for that photo! I was in heaven and knew what I had to do.

I called my husband and told him about it and said I wanted to buy it. He didn't argue with me because he knew how much I loved Elvis. Our entire game room and half the house was covered in Elvis memorabilia. I put in an offer on the house that day!

I couldn't believe that this house had not been memorialized! Why doesn't anyone know that Elvis lived here? I started to put a plan in place to turn it into a museum and a place with all the photos and memorabilia from when Elvis was in the army. The offer was accepted, and a few weeks later, I owned the home that Elvis lived in while he was in basic training (at Fort Hood, then called Camp Hood) in 1958. I began to decorate, and friends emerged and started to help make it a beautifully staged home full of Elvis's army memories. My plan was to decorate it and try to sell it to someone who was also a big Elvis fan with a lot of money who could turn it into something wonderful like it deserved to be!

I hired a company out of Tennessee that had just auctioned off a home that Elvis had lived in prior to his move to Killeen. That home appraised at around $80,000 and sold for nearly a million on eBay. The company was very excited to get the house and started marketing. We put it on eBay, and the results weren't as good as what we had hoped. We had a few celebrities who bid. We had bids up to our break-even point the day the auction ended and would've lost money to close on it. So we decided to put it up again at a later date.

During this downtime, I decided to have a party at the Elvis house. I invited about twenty-five of my closest girlfriends to spend the night there. We had a blast! Four or five different people were taking pictures that night, including me, when we had a realization.

In every picture that every person was taking with different cameras, there were orbs, anywhere from one to eighteen. So we began taking more and more pictures with all the different cameras at different parts of the house.

We ended up spooking ourselves out so badly that only five girls stayed to spend the night. When we finally turned out the lights, huddled together in our sleeping bags on the floor and got quiet, things got even weirder. Now, if you don't believe in the paranormal, you can choose to read this and dismiss it. But if you do believe in the paranormal, this was one of the creepiest experiences ever!

One of my friends suddenly yelled out, "What!"

I said, "What is it?"

She said, "One of ya'll keeps whispering my name! Stop!"

None of us had done it. We were all so truly freaked out and scared that out of respect for the other girls we weren't doing anything extra to scare each other that night. Right after that, another girl jumps up and screams, "Turn on the light!"

Someone turned on the light, and she was really upset and said that she had watched an orb float through the room into the kitchen. Only when it went around the corner did she have the breath or guts to say anything.

We talked about it for a while until we thought we were okay to go back to sleep. I had just gone back to sleep when I woke up to a weird pressure on me. I felt the sleeping bag pulling on one side and then I heard the zipper. I was frozen! My friend was dead asleep next to me and there was no one on my right. The zipper kept going and it unzipped about five or six inches before I screamed and wiggled out of the sleeping bag. It had stopped and my sleeping bag lay motionless. But that was it. We didn't sleep another wink that night.

We started to zoom in on the photos that we had taken and saw that the larger orbs had what looked like faces in them. One orb even had a gentleman with a top hat on and a frilly collar. In one picture, there was a woman holding a baby. You could see her arm perfectly with a pearl bracelet on, and she was holding a swaddled baby. You couldn't see the baby's face, but you could see her face. It was terrifying! After we had seen this photo with the lady with the pearl bracelet, we started finding these little pearls in every room of the house.

When morning came, we couldn't get out of there fast enough. I never went back into the house alone, again. I was really crept out. I don't know if any of these events had anything to do with Elvis, but to make things even weirder, Uri Gellar, the famous mentalist out of the UK, had expressed an interest in buying the home. He's most famous for bending spoons with his mind. His interest faded, and it didn't work out.

I ended up owning the home for two years, and I let anyone who was a fan go in and check out all the articles, photos, and memorabilia I had there. I became pregnant with our precious daughter and had a very rough pregnancy and nearly died after I gave birth. We had to let the house go and a very nice couple who are also Elvis Presley fans bought it. It tore me up inside to let it go. I wanted to be able to make sure that anyone who lived or came to Killeen would know that a music legend once lived here for a year and went to basic training at Fort Hood.

I learned of so many beautiful and interesting stories from people who had met him while he lived here. He was a kind man, kissed a lot of women who still live here, got clotheslined in a neighbor's backyard running from their dog while he was dodging crazed teens, and bitten by a dog that was in a parade with a sign around his neck that said, "I bit Elvis." He would just show up at bars and restaurants and would sing songs for them all night. There were many superstars who stayed there at the house and spent nights around the piano singing and laughing. His whole family and entourage lived there that year. That included his mother, Gladys, his father, Vernon, his grandmother, and his housekeeper/cook.

It was known that Elvis slept in a back room of the home that wasn't even a bedroom because girls would tap on the windows all night long. In fact, the whole reason he had to move to the house in town was because when he lived in the barracks at Fort Hood, it was an open base and girls ran through the barracks every night trying to find him, and no one could get any sleep.

The mayor of Killeen gave up his home to Elvis and his family and told them he could rent it out while he was here for boot camp training. The people of Killeen eventually found out that he was living there and crowds of people would wait in the street and in the driveway for him to drive up in his pink Cadillac. Every night, he would sign autographs, kiss babies and girls, and talk to the neighbors. On some occasions, he wanted to evade the crowd and would climb over all his neighbors' fences with their permission to get into his backyard. On one of these occasions is when he clotheslined himself, got knocked out, and woke up to the neighbors' dog licking his face!

There are many neighbors who still live there who remember Elvis very fondly. But none as fondly as an older gentleman and his wife whom I recently met at an open house I was holding in Killeen one hot summer Sunday afternoon. They said they had owned their home here since the fifties and were thinking that they needed a change, finally.

I asked them, "Well, I guess you got to see Elvis? He was here in 1958."

The wife instantly changed expressions to a forlorn look and held her gaze in her husband's eyes. He began to tear up. She talked for him because he couldn't talk. He was completely overcome with emotion. She said, "My husband was Elvis's staff sergeant in the army. They became very close friends."

I told her how I had bought the home that Elvis had lived in and how much it had meant to me. We were all crying at this point when finally the husband spoke.

He said, "Elvis was a good boy. He was dealing with things that no boy his age should have had to deal with. We talked a lot. He was my friend. When he was through with basic training here at Fort Hood, he was assigned to Germany. I went with him in the same group. He invited me up to his house that he had rented in Germany, and I'll never forget what he said. We were standing on a balcony one night overlooking a party at his house and he looked at me with so much sadness and with a wavering voice he said, "I don't know who any of these people are. Except you. Thank you."

As he finished his story, his eyes were full of tears and he was lost in a world that was still playing out in front of him. As I write this and remember the look on his face, I know exactly what type of person Elvis was and just how he affected everyone whom he was in contact with. He died three years after I was born, yet I have been enamored with him since I was able to talk. I would've given anything to have met him, to have heard him sing, or seen him smile. At least for a little while, I owned something that was special to him, where he spent his family time. And that is as close as I'll come. That's enough. Long live the King.

PART III
Military Matters

"No one is more cherished in this world than someone who lightens the burden of another. Thank you."

—Author unknown

THE GREATEST THANK YOU

A couple of years ago, I was introduced to a gentleman in his late sixties. He was a Korean War veteran and wore his hat that stated it so very proudly every day. He wanted people to know what he had gone through for our country's freedom, and I'm so glad because some of the things he told me that happened, I didn't know and I know others don't know and people have forgotten.

Agent Orange had been used when Mr. Monroe was fighting, and his body was slowly becoming harder for him to handle and control. He had a few ticks and health issues that were extremely hard to medicate or help. My heart went out to him. He told me that he needed to get his wife out of their current living situation and into a much better one. He said he wasn't expecting much because he had talked with some agents and friends who didn't paint a pretty picture for him because of his small retirement income.

I asked Mr. Monroe if he was granted any percentage of disability when he left the military. He said that they gave him 100 percent disability status because of how Agent Orange had ravaged and continued to ravage his body. I asked him if anyone had explained the benefits of being 100 percent disabled in the state of Texas. He said no. I couldn't believe it! We had just passed a law that veterans who were 100 percent disabled never had to pay property taxes ever again! Yes! Ever again! I explained to him how that changed everything and brought his monthly payment down to be affordable for his income. He had no idea. He started to cry.

At that moment, I almost wished that I hadn't gotten him so excited about it because he was positive that I was an angel who was going to help him and his wife get out their horrible rent house and into a beautiful, new, and clean home. He prayed and asked me to pray with him, and he thanked God for bringing someone into his life who was willing to help. I told him I would do everything I possibly could to get him into a better situation. That was the least he deserved for defending our country and slowly dying an agonizing death because of it.

Mr. Monroe told me about Mrs. Monroe. She had a horrible degenerative disease that had her bedbound. As weak as Mr. Monroe was, he would lift his wife out of bed, get her to her wheelchair, take her to the bathroom and back, wash her every day, feed her, sing to her, and lay down beside her for comfort. She was in terrible pain and on pain medication that just took the edge off. They were so in love with each other. He cried when he introduced me to her as she lay in her bed. The conditions they were living in were a travesty considering what he has done for this country. They deserved so much more. And their devout Christianity and undying positive attitude made me determined as I've never been before to get them out of there.

Loving this woman had become Mr. Monroe's calling and what he lived for. He always called her his "light" and his "love." When he was around her, he sang and she hummed. It was like listening to angels. I've never seen such love between two people before. He loved to help her and looked forward to helping her with the most menial tasks.

Mr. Monroe had no money. He lived month to month, but he always paid all his bills and had excellent credit. He got qualified for a home loan, and we all were so excited! He was on his way!

I was met with the difficult task of trying to find a home that had wide doorways, large open kitchen, large open master, and a large open bathroom so that his wife could maneuver down the hallways and through doorways in her wheelchair. There were no American Disability Association-approved homes on the market, and no builder was willing to change the floor plan to help Mr. Monroe.

I found a home that was ready and on the ground and only a couple of doorways needed to be widened and a ramp put into each entrance to the home. The builder wouldn't change it. They would not help. I was sick with despair. This was as close as we could find.

So I took matters into my own hands. I'm not giving up on these sweet people. I called the contractors who had been loyal to me and done great jobs for my previous clients. I got quotes to see how much it would be to make the changes after he closed on the house. It was quite a bit. I knew Mr. Monroe didn't have the money to do it, but I had to get him out of that house.

I met Mr. Monroe at the new house and walked him through and showed him what needed to be done and that I already had someone set up to do it the day he closed because the builder would not do it for us. He began to cry because he said he didn't have the money to pay for these repairs. He said, "You found us the perfect house. You are our angel. I can't leave my wife there. What do we do?"

I began to cry because I knew he genuinely needed a change. I told him that I would donate my commission at closing to pay for the changes to the house. It would only take three days to make the changes and then they could move in. I thought he was going to faint.

He cried, "Why are you doing this for us? We don't deserve this."

I hugged him and told him that he deserved so much more than what I could give them. It was payment enough for me to see him and his wife enjoying their new home.

We closed on his home, got the repairs done, widened the doors, poured the ramps, and rearranged the bathroom so his wife had room to maneuver around. Three days later they moved in, and it was the first time Mrs. Monroe had seen the home. He wheeled her around and they both cried as they sat in the kitchen. She put her hands to her face and said, "Praise God. This is really our home," as happy tears streamed down her beautiful face.

She easily made her way throughout the entire home and was so thankful and so excited and loved every single aspect of it. She said it was perfect and Mr. Monroe could not have been happier. His light, his love had a beautiful place to call home. All was well.

I came back to visit them a week later, and Mrs. Monroe had gotten worse. She was lying in her bed and she was in pain, but her sweet spirit and hospitality abounded. She asked me to come and sit on her bed, she held my hand, looked me in the eye with tears threatening to spill over and said, "Thank you."

To this day, that was better than any commission check I've ever earned; no other thank you has even come close to the genuineness of this woman. I cried and said, "You are welcome." We sat there and talked about children and plans for the future and how wonderful her husband was and how exciting it was to finally have a beautiful home to call their own. I hugged her goodbye, told her how much she meant to me, and that they can call me anytime for anything they need.

Their love was like a fairy tale. His dedication to her was only matched by his dedication to our country, and he had given so much and finally after all these years was able to get a little bit back. After meeting the Monroe's, I have decided to give something back to every military veteran that I help. I think it's the least I can do to thank our brave military men and women. Many people say thank you for my help, but the thank you that came from the Monroes will forever be the single most special moment in my real estate career.

Today, when we think of our military, we think of our brave active men and women who are putting their lives on the line. Let us not forget our veterans of foreign wars, military personnel, and prisoners of war who risked their lives years ago. They're still living out the terrors of those days long ago in their own way. Don't forget about these men and women. They deserve our respect and they deserve for us to respect and remember them; most of all. I will never forget Mr. Monroe. I hope that he gets the happiness that he deserves. He gave everything he had for you and for me—for our freedom.

ALL THE MONEY
IN THE WORLD

Most of the time, you don't expect to be inspired or completely awestruck on any given day. You get up every morning, brush your teeth, put your clothes on, and walk out the door for another vanilla day at work. Being here in Killeen, close to Fort Hood, has given me a chance to meet the strongest and bravest individuals I know I'll ever meet in life.

When my husband began his career as a firefighter, I would stay up the nights he was on shift and pray for him to come back home safely. Nearly ten years later, I'm still doing it but with my daughter now. "Please take care of Daddy. Watch over him and bring him home safely to us in the morning. Amen."

Until I moved here to Killeen and started to really see what life was like for these families, I didn't realize how lucky I have it. My husband works twenty-four hours, and then he's off for forty-eight hours. To me and my daughter, that twenty-four-hour stretch is excruciating, and we just want Daddy home with us. These military families go without their mommies and daddies for twelve to eighteen months at a time! Some daddies miss the birth of their sons and daughters, some mommies and daddies miss the first steps, the first words, the first day of school, or just being able to watch them grow and to hug them every day.

The military moms and dads are across the world, fighting for our freedom and are occasionally getting to speak to their loved ones on the phone or web. No one can know what's it's like for our soldiers over there. We know they come back changed. No one can know what it's like for the families who are here without their loved ones. Not knowing if they're safe tonight, or any night.

Some of the strongest women I've ever known have been military wives who somehow take care of everything that needs to be taken care of, be everywhere that all the kids have to be, and somehow retain their sanity and give all of their love to their children and to their significant other across the phone or Internet and still find time to support other families and friends in need.

I met one of these strong military wives one day as I was selling homes for a local builder. Two women walked into the model home; one was obviously the mother and the other the daughter. They looked so much alike. The daughter came in and did not raise her head but looked at the floor. She looked to be in her late twenties or early thirties. The mother was definitely the leader and began a conversation with me. She told me that her daughter and she would like to find two homes: one for her and her husband and one for their daughter. They wanted to live next to each other. They had a very close family.

I realized after about thirty minutes that the daughter had still not said a word and she couldn't even look at me. The mother was friendly and told me a lot about what they were looking for, but I could tell there was something else they were holding back.

So I took them to look at a few homes; the mother said she liked two but never asked the daughter what she liked. They exchanged a couple of painful glances, but that was about it. I tried to start conversations with the daughter, to break the silence and awkwardness, but the mother would interrupt and start on a different topic. I knew that we had the right homes for them, in the right location and the right price. The mother gave me their contact information and left with me telling them that I would call them tomorrow.

I sat in my office and just thought about that entire two and half hours of interaction. Not a single word from the daughter. Maybe she had emotional problems or physical problems. I didn't want to guess, but I knew that I needed another piece of the puzzle. So after they left, I began to write them a thank-you note and the thank you turned into a longer letter about how much I enjoyed helping them and how I wanted to make sure they found something perfect for their family because I could tell their daughter meant the world to them.

Two days later, the mother and daughter showed up again in my model, with a baking tin full of brownies. The daughter was still staring at the floor, but I saw that she had the letter I had written them in her hand. The mother handed me the brownies and said, "We've been a lot of places to look at homes. This will be a special deal, and we feel like we can trust you. No one else cared to spend the time or to write us a letter. We'd like to show our appreciation with these brownies, and we'd also like to build our homes with you."

She started to tear up a little and handed me the brownies. I thanked her, and we all sat down in my office and ate brownies and drank coffee. The mother suddenly said, "I don't know when my daughter will want to speak up. She's been through a terrible experience that we won't get into right now. But I can tell you what she would like in her new home until she feels up to talking."

I still had no idea what was going on, but I knew this sweet girl had gone through some sort of trauma. She still had not looked me in the eye or even mumbled a word. At the moment, she sat eating her brownie; and while her mom talked, she paused and stared ahead of her.

Suddenly the daughter put her brownie down. Without looking up and without moving, she said, "Thank you for not asking me to talk. Thank you for not asking what was wrong with me or why I'm so quiet. Thank you for your letter."

Then she looked me right in the eyes with tears rolling down her cheeks and said, "My husband was suffering from post-traumatic stress disorder in Iraq, and he killed himself. He was my soul mate. He was my life. I wasn't there for him when he needed me. I couldn't help him when he needed help. I was here, safe. He was there, sad and suffering. I don't have a husband. I won't ever get to have his children."

At this, she stopped and lost control. The mother put her arm around her daughter as if to say, "That's enough." But the daughter wanted . . . needed to go on.

With anger this time, she said, "The only reason I can buy this house is because my husband is dead! I have to use the money I got from his death! I would give back every penny and everything I have to get him back today!" She screamed, "This house will always remind me that he will not be here to share it with me." And with those final words, she broke down and cried a long overdue cry that sounded like relief and at the same time absolute despair.

We all sat together and cried and prayed. I helped build two houses for these unbelievably strong women. There were happy days and there were sad days. But family sticks together, and its love knows no bounds. That was several years ago, and they still live next to each other in the same homes I sold them. Only now, the daughter has found a husband, and there's a beautiful baby who lights up their home. It's not the family that she had originally planned, but it's a wonderful sight for me to see her running in her front yard, chasing her little toddler. Happy and full of love again.

If you ever need a moment to put things in perspective when you wake up every morning, thinking about how bad your day is . . . be thankful for your family, for undying love, for a God who takes care of us even in the bleakest and darkest of days and for the fact that you are alive.

Wherever you are, when you see a soldier, thank them; buy their lunch or just shake their hand. They deserve happiness and respect. The reason we can get up in the morning, go to work, be free, happy, and safe is because they are protecting us. There are thousands of families who would gladly give everything they have to get their loved ones back who have given their lives for our freedom. Thank you, soldiers and military heroes, for an army strong.

PART IV
Partner Parables

I've had many sales partners and trained sales agents over the years, and I've loved them all dearly. They were all so different in their own special ways, and I've never forgotten all the stories that have made me laugh uncontrollably and unfortunately wet my pants on several occasions. Here's a collection of short stories about my beloved partners and sales agents over the years.

A Blast of a First Day

It is my first day at my new neighborhood and also my first official day with a very large builder, and I meet my new partner. She's very pretty and outgoing and has a skirt on with some cute little heels. As she's showing me around the model homes, we get to the option and color selection room upstairs and she says, "Oh. This is really important. Shh. Listen."

Then she grabs her dress, pulls it up to her waist, throws her foot in the air, jumps up and farts so loud that it scares me and I jump.

"So. Any questions about the colors and options?" she says without even smiling or missing a beat.

"You just jump farted. I don't even know you," I said.

"Oh, that. Yep. Get used to it."

"I think I love you," I said. And we lived happily ever after and she's still one of my best friends.

FIRST DAY JITTERS

Several years later, I was working for a different company and a new girl had her first day as a new homes consultant. She said that she was a nervous person and that she took an extra dose of her anti-anxiety pill that morning. I was thinking that this wasn't a very good start but began to train her anyway.

I could tell she was very nervous because she kept running to the bathroom. She went to the bathroom about ten times in the matter of the first hour. She just kept saying how nervous she was. I told her it would be okay, that I used to be a teacher and I've been a sales trainer, I'm very patient and will help her through this. She tentatively agreed and kept working on the computer. Every once in a while, I would smell something foul and pretended not to smell it so her nerves wouldn't get any worse than they were.

Suddenly, she sprang up from her chair, looked at me with tears in her eyes, and cried, "I'm sorry!"

"For what?" I said quizzically.

"I thought that I just had to toot and I just crapped my pants big-time!" She started crying profusely.

I didn't know what to say and just sat there with my jaw on the floor. She didn't move, but the smell suddenly hit me, and I yelled, "Oh god! You're going to have to go home, I think."

"Yeah. It's a big one. It's diarrhea. And it's going down my pants leg." She bellowed and wailed in embarrassment.

"Go home! I won't tell. Change clothes and come back."

So she walked slowly to her car with a stiff-legged walk of shame, and we were partners for a year, and I've never told a soul until now.

POLITICALLY INCORRECT

Since I had teaching, sales training, and sales management experience, I was called on to train most all of the new salespeople. Some were young and soaked everything in and were excited to learn; and some were older, set in their ways, and said things that made you want to crawl under a rock.

The latter is the case of this story. One gentleman who I was training was on his fourth day and he was starting to get the hang of things by watching me greet customers and answer any questions about the neighborhood that people might have. On this day, I was writing a contract with another customer and I let the newbie greet people who came in. There is no better practice than to just do it!

I'm listening to the newbie greet a customer when they asked about the racial makeup of the community. Oh no! We haven't gone over a prepared response for that yet! Oh god! I jumped up to intervene but not quick enough. Now . . . my newbie has no issues with any race, but he has an issue with nervously saying things that he shouldn't and not remembering how or why he said it. I call it "information vomiting with no recall" or "The Bill Clinton Syndrome."

To the customer's question of racial makeup for the community, my newbie, obviously rattled and nervous spouts off, "Well . . . I can tell you immigration isn't staking out *this* neighborhood!"

Oh god! It was so painful. I ran out of my office and said, "I'm sorry. What he meant to say is that we're a beautifully diverse neighborhood, and we urge you to spend time in the neighborhood to find a home and atmosphere that works best for you and your family."

The newbie said, "Yeah. That's what I said," and looked at me like I was out of my mind for breaking in on his perfectly normal conversation.

REALISTIC PORTRAYAL
OF MODEL HOMES

I trained a company's sales team with a sales agent who had serious issues with drinking. I never said anything because I knew that it was so bad, that basically anyone could see it any time. Realtors began complaining that he was drunk and just handed them a key and went back to sleep at his desk. One realtor even told a story that he took them out to see a home, got out of the car, barfed on the street, wiped his mouth with his shirt and staggered into an inventory home to show them. She was mortified!

His last day of work, he had come in completely drunk. He opened the door to the model and passed out on the bed in the master's bedroom. He probably would have gotten away with it except the front door was open and a customer came in, tried to wake him, called 911, and the ambulance drove him to the hospital where he was treated for alcohol poisoning.

When asked about the ordeal, the customer said, "At first I just thought that it was some sort of new thing that showed you how real people can live in the models. I just thought he was acting. Then I got scared because I thought he was dead."

SUPER PARTNER STRENGTH

When you're a woman in real estate, you're always on edge when you're alone in an office or home with a stranger. This particular day, my partner and I were both working and a strange man walked in and started talking to Leslie, my partner. I immediately got a bad feeling when the hairs on my neck and arms stood on end. The questions he was asking seemed rehearsed. He asked to see the model home.

Leslie took him down the walk to see the model home. Another customer came in and I was busy for a little while with him and realized after he left that it had been a very long time and Leslie still wasn't back. I instantly felt scared and knew I was about to walk in on a bad scene. Every hair on my body was standing up as I opened the front door to the model home. I was right.

They were both at the top of the stairs. Leslie was crying and pleading with the large man to let her go and she was writhing but couldn't shake his grip. Something went through me that I've never felt before and I instantly was filled with unshakable bravery and strength and screamed, "Hey (bad word here)! Let go of her!"

The huge stranger was so transfixed by Leslie that he didn't even hear me and didn't see me charging up the stairs toward him. Leslie was about to pass out from fear and he was holding her up against him. I pushed through them and broke up his grip on her and Leslie fell to the ground crying. I burned a hole through his retinas and screamed, "Get out!"

What looked back at me was pure evil, and he smiled a sinister smile and started to move toward me, and I pushed him down the stairs. He fell down about six or seven stairs when he grabbed the rail, steadied himself, looked back up at me, and smiled again. I came after him and pushed him down the final flight and when he got up at the bottom of the stairs, it was like he had woken up from a dream or some sort of possession.

He looked at me like he'd never seen me before and said, "What the heck are you doing? What's wrong with you?" he asked indignantly and dusted himself off, stood up and said, "Ya'll are crazy." Then he left.

Immediately, the super human strength left and I felt extremely weak and didn't know if I could stay upright. I didn't know if I could make it up the stairs to check on Leslie or not. Somehow, I pulled myself up and called out to her and she said she was okay. I made it to the top of the stairs and hugged her as we both sat on the ground and cried, both weak from fear.

She said, "Thank you. I was so scared. I don't know what he would have done to me."

"That's what partners do." I said. "We watch out for each other's backs."

I had never seen that guy before and thankfully I never saw him again. I don't know what came over me that day, but I think I was possessed too. But definitely not with the same spirit he was possessed with. A spirit that was strong enough to ward off pure evil.

MY SILLY SALLY

My partner for a while, Sally, had a way with words. The way was incorrectly using those words and other phrases that would have me rolling in laughter and have other people looking at her like she had lost her mind!

Every morning, Sally and I drove through Starbucks and got a coffee and a scone. We ended up getting these little miniscones and a whole bag full of them at that. She'd never had a scone until I introduced them to her. So after we had driven through, we went to our meeting to write a contract with a buyer and local builder. The sales representative for the local builder asked us if we wanted anything to eat or drink. Sally said,

"Oh my gosh, no! We just ate about four *sconces*!"

My Silly Sally Continued

Sally and I were in a local store together shopping for a last-minute Valentine card for my husband. I had worked so late that day that I had to browse through the picked-over cards to bring him something home at the last minute. So she was helping me quickly look over them by reading aloud the first few lines to see if it would work for me and my husband. We're not really too mushy, so most of them we'd read aloud and then said, "Oh no! Not even close! That's stupid!"

So we're both reading cards aloud, and she pulls one out and says, "Hey! Tah-dah! Ummm . . . *this* card sucks."

She puts the card back in the slot and continues to look. I'm still shopping, but I stopped to think about that card she just picked up and what she had just said. I was interested. "Hey! Tah-dah!" just seemed like a weird way to start a Valentine card.

So I go over and pick up this "Hey, Tah-dah!" card and start to read it. It's in Spanish, and it really reads, "Hoy Toda . . . ," which in Spanish means "Today everything." Of course at that point I just have to hand her the card, sit in the aisle, and hold myself because I already know I've peed a little.

At this very moment, a well-respected local builder sales representative walks through the door and sees me holding myself, sitting in the aisle howling and Sally doubled over, holding her stomach and crying laughing. There's no telling what she truly thinks about us now.

TERRIBLE TORI
CAN'T TELL A STORY

Since Tori was a new agent and her first listing appointment didn't go so well, I decided to give her another try. Years ago, I sold a house to a nice couple and they were ready to sell it and buy another home. So we had a great listing appointment and great conversation. Tori hadn't said anything crazy the whole night.

We decided that we would list the home soon and get things moving. As we were leaving, I complimented them on how beautiful their wood floors were and how perfectly shiny and meticulous they were. I asked the owners how they got them that clean and the husband said, "Well . . . I just let my wife do it because I can't ever get it as clean and spotless as she can."

I said, "Well, I'm sure that your wife puts more love into the work than you." Everyone chuckled and then Tori had to add her two cents. I think that Tori was just trying to add to the conversation in a funny way, but it turned out to be explicit and made everyone uncomfortable.

After I commented that the homeowner can't get the floors as clean as his wife can without the love she puts into it, Tori bends her knees, gyrates her hips, and moves her hand around in a really disgusting manner and says, "I guess you just need to give it a little *love rub!*"

When she says "love rub," she bent her knees more, really got into it with her hand in a circle, and put a gritty inflection in her voice.

Silence.

I just looked at her, shocked, and said, "Go to the car."

Tori said, "What?" and then realized she must've done it again and resigned herself to sit in the car. I said the goodbyes to the clients and came and sat next to her in the car. She knows that she said something horrible but really doesn't have a clue what it was.

I say, "Do you know that you just gyrated and *grittily* told them to try a little *love rub?*"

Then we both fell out and I wasn't able to drive away for a good ten minutes. I never took Tori with me again. She's an amazing realtor but knows to stick to just business. When she starts to try comedic banter, it fails with hilarious results.

Taxes: What a Pain in the Rear!

One of my new partners in training was trying to tell a customer that taxes were paid "in arrears" but this is what she said:

"Yeah. Taxes are paid in the rear."

Strangely . . . her clients agreed.

Bionically Speaking

One of my older, more seasoned agents was trying to tell my assistant and me that if she could speak another language, she needed to speak Ebonics so she'd be up with all the new slang that she didn't understand. That's what she tried to say. This is what she actually said:

"I really wish I could speak bionics."

Part V
Shorties but Goodies!

Some stories deserve pages and pages to describe their hilarity. These short stories are hilarious and quickly get to the ridiculous point! I hope you laugh as hard as I did when each of these events happened.

Sorry, It's the Flux Capacitor

One of my construction managers was having a hard time communicating with an Asian couple who were continually calling in for warranty service on the weirdest things, and they spoke very little English. They'd call in saying the blind strings that pull the blinds open were too long or too short or that the front door doesn't swing just right. The manager could never get them to understand exactly what he was going to have to do to fix it or how to explain that he couldn't fix it and that was something normal.

So what he ended up doing every time was telling them that the "flux capacitor" wasn't working right and he wasn't able to fix it. They seemed to know that the "flux capacitor" could be an issue and were okay with that and somehow accepted that a "flux capacitor" was attached to nearly everything in the house, and it went out a lot.

The flux capacitor was *not* covered by our warranty.

(If you need help with the term *flux capacitor*, Google it along with the movie *Back to the Future*.)

Yes, I Hid Under My Desk from My Customers

I used to hide under my desk once a week and lock all the doors to the model home when a local lady who lived in the neighborhood used to bring over the worst tasting food I've ever put in my mouth. She wouldn't leave until I had eaten it all, and I would literally be stifling gags and smiling to not hurt her feelings. She would try the front door, side door, back door, model doors, and knock on all the windows trying to get in so I'd have to eat that nauseating food. I liked her and didn't want to hurt her feelings, but I can't eat that!

She would call and I would tell her how sorry I was that I always seemed to miss her when she came by with food and that it's a shame because it's *so* good. I know. I'm horrible.

Construction Workers DO Give a Crap!

Construction workers in our neighborhoods, and I'm sure it's probably rampant everywhere, used to take great comedic pleasure in taking a dump in nearly every part of the home they were building. They would crap in the attic making special and extremely precise aim at a roof truss that was two inches wide. They would crap between the wall and the sheetrock so no one could get to it except to tear out the sheetrock. Kitchen sinks were a normal occurrence. Once, a team of construction workers somehow got poop on kitchen faucets, sprayers, towel holders, and toilet holders and then they filled the bathtub up with water and left floating gifts in there. I'm sure they thought they were especially creative.

On several occasions, we had clients who would see it and would not buy the house until the toilet and the bathtub were removed and replaced! I would want the same thing! If you're building a home, check everywhere, every day. You never know when the person building your home will leave you an early house warming gift!

What a Dump!

Speaking of crap, about a year ago, I was showing some clients a few foreclosures in the area. I knew upon opening the door to one of the foreclosures that the listing realtor had *not* gone inside the home but instead just put the sign up and a picture of the outside. If he had made some sort of effort, he would have saved me adding to the mess inside with my own vomit.

Now, it's commonly known that when people leave the home that the bank has foreclosed on, the ex-owners don't really care about the shape it's in. They're steaming mad at the bank that has taken their home from them, and they'll take anything that's not strapped to the house down to all the appliances, ceiling fans, light switches, window blinds, carpet, and sometimes even granite countertops and cabinets!

This time, the ex-owner must have been *very* mad at their bank because they left a deposit in every single room of the house. When my clients and I walked through the door of this home, we were immediately smacked in the face with a foul smell. As we went in further, we saw a gigantic pile of crap in the living room. We dismissed it as a wild animal or dog that had gotten in and did it until we continued . . . and in *every* room of this home, the ex-homeowner had taken a crap on the floor.

On the third one, when I realized what it was, I threw up in my mouth and ran outside to vomit, slightly missing the outdoors! It was seriously the most disgusting thing I've ever seen. No self-respecting realtor wants that listing!

So I called the listing realtor and told him what we found. He acted like it wasn't a big deal and said, "The house is being sold 'as is.' It's a great deal; do your clients want it?" I was shocked.

That house is still referred to as "The Piece of Crap House." Realtors! Walk your listings! You don't want to list a dump!

WE WANT THE
CRAZY CAT LADY HOUSE!

Recently, I took the cutest young couple out to look at foreclosures in a really low-price range. As long as you have a little cash to fix them up, you can get a pretty good deal, and they were excited to go look. The first house we came to in my opinion was the worst house I'd ever seen. When we opened the door, the smell of ammonia (cat urine) just about knocked us out. My eyes immediately started watering, and I could actually see a yellow cloud in the room. It was awful!

Upon further examination, the carpet was no longer carpet but a one-inch pile of cat fur compacted with decades of urine stains. The ammonia cloud had actually painted the walls a putrid shade of dingy yellow. Where the pictures used to be on the walls were perfect rectangles and squares of white where the urine cloud didn't absorb into the wall. The ceiling was falling in, and it was raining inside the kitchen.

After seeing a few other houses that weren't quite as bad, my clients decided on the home with cat fur carpet and urine-painted walls. They liked the layout and thought they could slowly clean it up. We went back to take a look, and it was worse the second time around, but they wanted it.

My husband could smell the ammonia on me when I got home that night, and I showed him the pictures, and he couldn't believe it. It just goes to show you, a little . . . er . . . a lot of cat pee may be just what some people are looking for. Trust me, no matter how horrific it is . . . *any* house can sell!

THE WORD OF THE DAY
IS . . . JOB

O ne day, a nice man walked into my office, and we talked about him buying a home for his small daughter and himself. Once we started to talk about the money situation, I asked, "What's your occupation?"

With a scrunched up face he said, "What? Occa-puh . . . what? I don't know what you're asking."

I said, "Your occupation? Your *job*?"

"Oh! Well, why didn't you say so? I'm a trucker."

Just Get Out!

Late one evening when I was about to pack up and leave the model home, one of my clients came in and wanted to discuss some issues. So we started up a little paperwork and he started to squirm in his chair. I didn't understand why he was squirming until the green cloud of death hit me.

I couldn't help it. As professional as I tried to be, I jumped up out of my chair and yelled, "Dude! Are you serious? That's the worst thing I've ever smelled!"

He got up slowly and said, "I was hoping you wouldn't smell it. I'm sorry. I've been taking some weird medicine and it's so bad that even I can't stand it. I'm sorry. Let's leave."

I said, "Just in case it follows you, why don't I just email you the documents?"

He conceded since I was dry heaving and left.

CRAZY, TATTOO CLOWN FACE

I was selling houses in a new community that was really out in the country and away from everything. I was selling out of a temporary trailer home and selling high-end homes at the lake. People rarely came out there unless I had invited them or had an advertised special. It was hard to sell high-end homes out of a trailer home, but it was the most successful year of sales I ever had.

One summer day, I had just gotten through showing homes to a very large man in overalls with a giant beer gut, cowboy hat, and unlighted cigar in his mouth. The spitting image of Boss Hogg from *The Dukes of Hazzard*. He really liked one of the homes that I showed him and said that he wanted his wife to see it because she made all the decisions. So we parted ways, and I said I'd call him and see when his wife could come by to look at it. I told him I was headed to a lunch date anyway.

Just a few minutes later, I was sitting in my truck in front of the trailer home, texting my lunch date about to leave when the most terrifying face I've ever seen popped up into my open window! It had crazy black hair, tattooed eyebrows, tattooed eyeliner, tattooed lip liner, and clownlike rouge on its cheeks. I say "it" because at this point I was so scared by this face, an inch away from mine that I couldn't even think!

The scary, tattooed clown face said in a voice that you'd swear was the witch in the *Wizard of Oz*, "I scare you?"

Out of straight adrenaline-powered fear, I screamed bloody murder and yelled, "Yes!"

She said she was the wife of the gentleman that I just showed houses to. I later learned that she was from Korea. But she then said to me, with her scary face still an inch from mine in the window, "You no go nowhere. You no eat lunch. You show us home . . . you still scared?"

I nodded yes and she laughed a crazy *Wizard of Oz* wicked witch laugh, walked back to her car, and waited for me to show them their new house.

SHART

I was showing homes to a customer late one afternoon. We were standing on the back patio of a home and he farted really loud. So loud that he jumped and I jumped and we said "Oh!" at the same time.

He said, "I'm sorry!"

I laughed and said "Don't worry. I've heard it all before." I didn't want him to feel self-conscious and I mainly wanted to forget it ever happened.

"Well, you're lucky," he said.

"I am?" I said. Ugh. Here we go.

"Yeah. Usually s_ _t shoots out. I've been a little 'off' when it comes to my bowels lately," he said apologetically but obviously not ashamed to let me know his gastric secrets.

Shocked, I was still trying to make light of it by shrugging it off, but he just kept adding to the description, making it more awkward and pretty disgusting.

I said, "So is it like a shart? I'm sorry. That sounds like a horrible affliction."

He said, "No. I wish they were like sharts. These are full on 'dump your pants' farts!"

Silence.

EPILOGUE

Literally days before I had to turn in the manuscript for this book, I was leaving the office at dusk, laden with a huge computer bag and an even heavier purse. I was right in front of my car with some clients of the brokerage heading to their car as well. I took a step with my right foot and suddenly I was literally sprawled on my stomach and in so much pain that I couldn't breathe!

My ankle had turned (again) so badly that it came out of socket and my foot was stuck in a ninety degree angle, completely out, and hanging grossly to the side! I was on my stomach, holding my right leg in the air because I couldn't put it down with my foot completely popped out and radiating excruciating pain. I literally wasn't breathing, it hurt so badly.

The clients now hovering over me were yelling at each other trying to figure out how to help me. They were convinced that I was having a seizure. I *was* holding a pretty weird pose to keep my foot off the ground!

Holding this ridiculous pose, without breathing, in horrific and epic pain, I realized that my foot was not going to pop back in by itself. The only thing I could do was start pounding it against the concrete to get it to go back in. So after about three hard blows, it rolled back into the socket. Fortunately, I was in a little less pain, just enough to breathe, cry, and writhe in agony.

By this time, the people from the business next to us and everyone in my office were standing around me staring at me. I don't think anyone knew what to do. The only word I could manage to yell out was, "Ankle!"

At least now, they knew I wasn't having a seizure. Luckily, the business next door to us sells supplements and the men who helped me were big muscled up men who were shopping for muscle enhancers. Two of them came over and picked me up, and even though they were large men, they were huffing and puffing from the exertion. I'm not petite.

They sat me on the couch in our office, and I realized that I had to go to the emergency room. Turns out, I had broken the tip off one of my ankle bones and had severe ligament damage, with surgery a definite on the horizon.

Only a couple of days later, while I was back in the office talking with my partner CJ, did he tell me that if it hadn't been for the muscled-up guys next door, there wasn't any way he was going to pick my big butt up. He said he would've just left me there and called 911. Then he made sure to mention that he wasn't going to treat me any different now that I can't get around. So he made me a special box for people to drop stuff in that needed to be taken care of or if I needed something they could just drop it in. He wrote "In-box" on it and taped it to my back. So that was a big help.

I love my career. I love my business partners, CJ and my husband. I love my clients. The thought that hundreds of families are happy in a home making memories right now and that I had a small part in making that happen makes it all worth it. Those soul-gripping, heartfelt thank-you's, the visits after they move in when the kids are running around, so excited to be in their new home—those are the times when my heart is overcome with happiness and the knowledge that I was led to the right place, at the right time, and to the right people.

I've been so blessed through the years to have amazing sales partners, managers, peers, and now my own brokerage with a world-class business partner. The days that I prayed for God to send me a sign seem so long ago now, but I know now without a doubt that because I asked for guidance, he gave it to me, and I'm in the place where I'm supposed to be.

I'm looking forward to the next ten years of stories as the co-owner of StarPointe Realty in Killeen, Texas. I'm looking forward to helping more families and helping our military heroes. I'm looking forward to writing book number 2! I hope that you have enjoyed this book as much as I have enjoyed living these experiences and reliving them through stories told and retold. I'll leave you with the picture taken just days before I submitted this book complete with crutches and my homemade *In-box*. My beloved partner CJ is so thoughtful! Until the next book, I hope you all remember to look at the *funny* in life and to ask God for guidance. You'll get your shining light that points you in the right direction. I did!

Myka Allen-Johnson has had a lifetime full of hilarious and outrageous experiences starting with being raised as a Baptist preacher's daughter. As a Christian, she was raised to see the beautiful side of life but also the *funny* side. Myka started her real estate career in new home sales and general real estate, then as the sales trainer for a Fortune 500 builder, and now as the owner of a successful real estate brokerage in Texas. She lives the fast paced life of a mom, wife and business owner but always takes time out for God and to enjoy life with a humorous view of the world that allows her to laugh . . . every day.

Follow the author:

Blog: http://mykajohnsontexasrealtor.blogspot.com

Facebook: www.facebook.com/talesfromsales

Twitter: @StarPointeMyka